The Sermons of

BEHOLD *your* GOD

Rethinking God Biblically

JOHN SNYDER

Cover design and text layout by Sarah J. Snyder.

Printed in the United States of America
ISBN 979-8-9857851-2-8

Special thanks to Virginia McCallum for her labors on this project.

Published by

MEDIA GRATIAE
P.O. BOX 21
NEW ALBANY, MS 38652
EMAIL: INFO@MEDIAGRATIAE.ORG

WWW.MEDIAGRATIAE.ORG

CONTENTS

Dedicated to my mother

ROBEE SNYDER

Whose words taught me about the God of Scripture
from my earliest days
and whose example has displayed His reality
in the years since.

INTRODUCTION

The careful student of the Bible might be surprised to find that true faith is not always a comforting thing. In fact, there are times when taking God at His word causes a person to be deeply troubled in a way that those who do not take God at His word are not.

This discomfort occurs when there is an apparent contradiction between the things we read in the Bible, regarding the activity of God and the privileges of His people, and the things you view in everyday life. When you go from the pages of the Bible to the morning news—from the lofty descriptions of the Christian life to your local church, from the biblical boasts in Jesus of Nazareth to your own sluggish and inconsistent responses to those passages—it can be alarming if you care.

Isaiah cared. Toward the end of his book, he compared God's apparent indifference to His people's moral decay to what he read in the Scripture of God's past actions. The gap between the biblical accounts and the present condition of God's people alarmed him. In fact, he was concerned to the point of asking a very significant question: "Where is He?" (Isaiah 63:11).

You may ask that same question as you move from the pages of your Bible to your home, workplace, or church. Is this poor dying rate of Christianity, which we too often (though thankfully not always) exhibit in western evangelical churches the best God that can do? Is He still with us at all?

It does not take an extraordinary measure of discernment to point out the decline of western religious culture and the accompanying moral ruin that is visible in people outside of church. Many have noticed and responded with helpful analysis. Books enough to fill your shelves have resulted from their literary response to this crisis. There does, however, seem to be a noticeable failure to get beneath the surface of things—even beneath the problems of wrong worldviews, systemic hypocrisy, and humanity's addiction to the fantasy of self-determination. What is at the root of these is the simpler problem of willful ignorance. Even in places where church buildings still exist in great number and are still filled on Sundays, an appalling ignorance of God reigns undisturbed. After all, nothing is easier in a church gathering than to assume that all those who are members think right thoughts when they hear the word "God." But what if we are blinded by our pride? What if the God that the Bible reveals is not the One whom we adore in our thoughts? What if being reintroduced to the God of the Bible is the one thing we need more than anything else? What if the influential 20th-century author and pastor, A. W. Tozer, was correct when he claimed that Christians will find the solutions to ten thousand lesser problems when they discover who God really is?[1] What if returning to the Bible and rethinking God according to the descriptions we find on its pages—that most delightful and frightening of spiritual tasks—is the correct starting place for restoring ourselves, our homes, our churches, and our nations?

The sermons in this book have been adapted to make them appropriate for reading. They were preached in 2012 as part of a Bible study entitled *Behold Your God: Rethinking God Biblically*. They were originally accompanied with a workbook in which the listener would find scriptural foundations for what was said. (This twelve-week study is still available for those who desire more than what is contained here.) For those who have not worked through the full study, this book of sermons has been published to provoke serious questions and to stir up the desire to know the God of the Bible as never before.

[1] A. W. Tozer, *The Knowledge of the Holy,* (New York: Harper Collins Publishers, 1961), 2

The end of all learning is to know God, and out of that knowledge to love and imitate Him.

JOHN MILTON

1

BEHOLDING GOD

The Great Attraction

After God brought the nation of Israel out of bondage in Egypt, they began their life of freedom with an astonishingly foolish choice. While Moses was with the one true God on Mount Sinai for forty days, the recently unfettered Israelites decided the best thing to do was to have a worship service in familiar Egyptian fashion. They convinced Aaron to build an idol—specifically, a golden calf. God was so displeased with this idolatrous choice that He threatened to destroy Israel. Moses then interceded with God on the mountain, and God promised mercy. Moses was not satisfied. He asked for more: "Please, show me Your glory" (Exodus 33:18).

When you consider the life of Moses, this is quite a surprising request. Hadn't Moses already seen the glory of God in a burning bush? Hadn't Moses already seen the glory of God demonstrated in ten powerful plagues, which humiliated the gods of Egypt and rescued the Israelites? Hadn't he already seen the Red Sea parted, the people of God brought over safely, and the armies of Egypt drowned? And yet, Moses wanted more.

Years later, a young king named David wrote, "One thing I have desired of the LORD, that will I seek: that I may dwell in the house of the LORD all the days of my life, to behold the beauty of the LORD" (Psalm 27:4). In the same Psalm, he wrote this: "When You said, 'Seek My face,' my heart said to You, 'Your face, LORD, I will seek'" (Psalm 27:8).

The desire to behold the beauty of the Lord, to seek His face, is not a desire that is confined to the Old Testament saints. The apostle Paul, thirty years after the ascension of Christ and decades after being conquered by His love, wrote, "Yet indeed I also count all things loss for the excellence of the knowledge of Christ Jesus my Lord, for whom I have suffered the loss of all things, and count them as rubbish, that I may gain Christ . . . that I may know Him" (Philippians 3:8,10). This mighty longing to know God more, to grow in an intimate and personal awareness of Him, is a common thread throughout the Bible.

The longing to know God doesn't stop with the end of Scripture. In the seventeenth century, a Baptist pastor named John Bunyan (who spent years in prison for the crime of preaching) wrote, "God is the only desirable good. Nothing without Him is worthy of our hearts. The life, the glory, the blessedness, the soul-satisfying goodness that is in God are beyond expression."[1] Later, in the mid-twentieth century, a pastor in Chicago named A. W. Tozer wrote this prayer in his book, *The Pursuit of God*: "Oh, God, I have tasted Thy goodness, and it has both satisfied me and made me thirsty for more. . . I want to want Thee. I long to be filled with longing. Show me Thy glory, I pray Thee, that so I may know Thee indeed." [2]

This unashamed pursuit of an intimate and personal knowledge of God, this mighty burden to know God better as a believer—a burden that cannot be lifted by anything less than one-on-one contact with our Creator—is the subject that we will explore.

Sadly, hearing words such as these about God may seem strange to us. We may think that these writers exaggerated. We may feel that they used poetic license when describing the greatness of God and the desire of their own hearts. We may feel that they let their emotions run away with them; but there is another possibility. The difference between what we see as "normal Christianity" and the picture of Christianity displayed by these believers may be rooted in the fact that they knew God in a way that we do not. But why would this be? Is their experience something we are meant to merely read about? Should we place this kind of experience in the realm of curious fiction that doesn't touch the reality of life? No. That kind of thinking is tragic and unnecessary. Neither God nor His Word have changed; therefore, we have no excuse for a half-hearted pursuit of Him.

As we search the Scriptures together, we want to seek the Lord the way they did. Like Moses, we want to plead with God, "Yes, You've given us favor in Christ. Please, show us Your glory." Like David, we come to God and desire to have responsive hearts: "When You say, 'Seek My face,' Lord, my heart says, 'Your face I will seek.'" Like Paul, we want to count all things, in comparison to knowing Christ, as garbage. Like John Bunyan, we want to be able to say, "I have tasted and found that God is so good that His goodness, His satisfying goodness, is beyond expression." And, like A. W. Tozer, we want to say, "We long to be filled with a holy longing that can only be met in Him."

Though the gap between what we experience as Christians and what we read of past saints' longings may be rooted in the fact that they knew God better, there is another and more grievous possibility: it may be that the God they knew was the God of the Bible and the God whom we hold in our minds is a god of our imagination. The idea that we have fashioned of God, even as believers, may be so far from biblical descriptions of Him that no one would ever say, "I count all things loss to know *that* God." No one would say, "Having been given favor, Oh God, show me Your glory." No one would set their heart to pursue the small and inadequate god that we have imagined. We want to make sure that it is the God of the Bible whom we are pursuing.

Passion is a word that is valued in modern Christianity. Passion, however, is not enough on its own. What is the value of being passionate about a god that doesn't exist? If we are passionate about a god of our imagination, if we are passionate about a god that has been passed down to us from our culture, but is not the God of the Bible, then our passion is worthless.

To set our hearts toward a right pursuit of the one true God, there are four basic truths that we must master. These truths will help us to understand and benefit from the Scriptures that contain God's self-descriptions. These are truths that we want to get a grip on, but they are also truths that we want to get a grip on us.

The first truth—if you really want to get to know God and to get a clear and biblical view of Him—is this: you must understand that the most significant thing about you is what comes to your mind when you think of the word *God*.[3] This truth applies to all people and not just to those who claim to be Christians. Every man, woman, and child will make choices based on his or her general idea of what God is like. Even an atheist has a type of religion based on the thought that God doesn't exist. And, based on his belief in the nonexistence of God, the atheist will make certain decisions. He makes certain decisions in his home; he makes decisions at work. The Muslim makes decisions based on *his* view of his god. The Christian makes decisions based on *his* view of his God. What you think of God is the most distinguishing thing about you. Education, ethnicity, age—none of these are so distinguishing as what you, deep down, really believe about God because that belief affects everything.[4] All desires, thoughts, and actions will flow from it.

So, what is your view of God? I'm not asking you what your official view of God is. I don't want a Sunday school answer. I don't want you to ask yourself, "What does my church say I'm supposed to believe about God?" I don't want you to ask, "What does my denomination say I should believe about God? What do the books on my shelf say I believe about God? What do my parents say that I should believe about God?" The question is: What do you really believe and think of when you think of God? Your true view of God is not as easy to spot as your denomination's views, creeds, or confessions.[5] Your true view of God might remain hidden under a huge pile of rubble made up of phrases you picked up from church or Christian podcasts. Your true thoughts of God may be hiding behind the words you say that sound good but mask what you actually believe. If you are going to really understand what you think about God, it will take a courageous and determined search of your heart.

The second truth is that knowing God is the great jewel of Christianity. Though we are thankful for the many other gifts that have come from the cross of Christ, those gifts all lead back to this great source—the knowledge of Christ Himself. Currently, even in churches, the idea prevails that knowing God is a casual and easy thing! Knowing Him is on the same level of relationship as bumping into a stranger and acknowledging his existence. For example, a child comes to the pastor and says, "I don't want to go to the hell that you've talked about. I want the heaven you talked about. I want the friends you talked about. I want the happiness you talked about." Those are all good things, and the pastor says (depending on the church tradition), "You need to join the church," "You need to get baptized," or "You need to repeat these words after me and ask Christ into your heart." These steps are taken, and the child is told that he or she now knows God. The implication is "Well done, child. That's it. That's the end of the journey." But this is an unbiblical view.

Because of the mistaken belief that knowing God is the easiest thing in the world, we take for granted that everyone in our church knows God. We sit down. We look to the left and to the right, and we see cleaned up, nice people. They are our friends and family. We really have a hard time imagining that anybody on the pew next to us, anyone in our small group, may not know God. Some of the consequences of this wrong view are the flippancy in our worship, the casualness with which we stroll up to God in our prayers, and the boredom that we display with the Bible unless the preacher is giving us four steps to happiness. In reality, knowing God is no small matter. I wonder, are we so casual with God because we in the twenty-first century know Him so well? Or is it because we hardly know Him at all?

Where are some of the Scriptures that teach us the magnitude of knowing God? The first is found in John 17:1–3, where Christ prays, "Father, the hour has come. Glorify Your Son that Your Son also may glorify You, as You have given Him authority over all flesh, that He should give eternal life to as many as You have given Him. And this is eternal life, that they may know You, the only true God, and Jesus Christ whom You have sent." Do you see what He says there? Did you catch that? "Father, You have given Me all the authority so that I can bring people to know You. And this is eternal life," not a long existence in paradise. Christ says that eternal life is knowing His Father and knowing Him. The significance of knowing God cannot be exaggerated. In order for a person like you, in order for a person like me, to know a God like that, God must entrust all authority into the hands of His Son, the God-man, as He goes to the cross. Anything less than that—anything less than all divine authority—is not enough to accomplish what had to be accomplished for us to know Him.

In Philippians 3, we see that knowing God has a beginning. In conversion, a person comes to Christ in a repentant faith. That person embraces Christ for who He is and lays at Christ's feet all that he or she is. But conversion is only the introduction to God. It's not the entire relationship. It's the beginning. Young couples who are getting married are not satisfied to come together for the marriage ceremony and then leave the building and never see each other again. Yet, that is the kind of Christianity we often accept and even promote. New converts are told, "Come, ask Christ to save you, trust Him to do that, and you are guaranteed heaven. If you want more, it would be good if you joined the church. It would be good if you worked. Put your shoulder to the wheel. Look at all these other Christians, giving, working for the Lord. Don't you want to be one of them?" If the convert should ask, "What about longing to know God better?," we assure them that they already have all the knowledge of God they need.

We may not actually say this to people, but our actions imply that the introduction to God is everything. What Paul teaches is so different. When he writes Philippians, he has known Christ for years. Who knows Christ better than Paul? Would any of us say, "I think that my experiences of God are probably more glorious than Paul's experiences in twenty years of ministry"? Who, like Paul, has seen the glory of Christ demonstrated in the way He conquered people, families, and cities? Who, like Paul, has a clear grasp of the doctrines of the Bible? He wrote half the books of the New Testament. And yet Paul in essence says to the Philippians, "If you want to know, really, what goes on inside of your pastor, I'll tell you. I'm still counting everything else as loss, even the good things in my past; I look away from them in order that I might have more of Christ. I want to know Him."

Another evidence that the knowledge of God is not insignificant is the fact that knowledge of God can flourish even in the worst spiritual environment. It is not in pleasant, easy circumstances where we find the knowledge of God growing. It is not in good churches only, nor just in the New Testament, where there seems to be a great revival of religion under the teaching of the apostles. It is not only when David is king and is pointing the nation to God. The opposite is more often true. People in the worst churches, in the worst families, living at the worst times, can cultivate a growing intimacy with the uncreated God.

Hosea, the prophet, preaches during a time when Israel is so idolatrous that God compares her to an adulterous wife who has been brought out of a filthy lifestyle. After living a while with a clean husband, she grows bored and bold and goes back to the old life. Over and over, she is brought back to her husband, but she leaves again. Hosea is sent to his wife with threatening messages, but in chapter six of the book of Hosea, he is sent with a message from God to entice her. The message to this adulterous woman is "Yes, God has torn us, but He will heal us. He's wounded us, but He will be merciful. He has withdrawn His presence, but He will come back." Verse three follows with the exhortation, "Let us know, let us press on to know the Lord. His going forth is as certain as the dawn; and He will come to us like the rain, like the spring rain watering the earth" (Hosea 6:3). Nothing can be compared to the jewel of knowing Him—really knowing Him—forever.

The third great truth is this: today, the truth that the knowledge of God is the great treasure of the Christian life has been replaced by pursuits of secondary matters. The early days of the twenty-first century have been days when (especially in the West) there has been a very aggressive rethinking of many aspects of Christianity. There has been a rethinking of worship styles, rethinking of inner-city church plants, rethinking of how we raise a family. It was good to rethink these issues. The changes that have occurred because of this rethinking are extreme, but the problem is that these changes are not truly radical. Radical means foundational or root level. No matter how much you change the worship style, no matter how differently you approach inner-city missions, no matter how differently you raise your family, no matter how extreme the changes in these external areas, they are not radical because we are not actually getting to the root problem that must be dealt with before the fruit of change can be lasting and pleasing to God.

All this rethinking deals primarily with the externals. When we consider pursuit of a high and biblical view of God, when we consider the duty of rethinking God biblically, we need what historian Mark Noll referred to as "a Copernican revolution."[6] Who was Copernicus? He was a Renaissance astronomer. Copernicus viewed the night sky and, with scientific precision, he recorded and studied the movements of the planets. He came to the revolutionary discovery that the earth is not the center of the solar system. It's not the center of the universe. While that fact may seem silly to us, it was news for his time. Sadly, the Roman Catholic Church—misinterpreting passages in the Bible—condemned the idea that the sun was the center of the solar system and that our earth was orbiting the sun. They said, "No, that doesn't sound right to us. We believe that God said in the Bible that the sun orbits the earth. The earth is the center." Of course, God did not say that, but because of previous mistaken beliefs, Copernicus's findings shook the Catholic church to its core.

We need—you need—a spiritual Copernican Revolution. You need to go to the Scriptures and study passages that describe God. You need to study them with as much precision and determination as Copernicus studied the night sky. Study them until you have a Copernican revolution. In our day, we have been told, even by the church, that we are the center of the universe. Me, my spiritual needs, my eternal destination—that is what is important. My family, my town, my friends, our church, our denomination, and our nation are the center of all creation. We must lovingly and humbly go back and say, "It's a lie." Everything in church, everything at home, and everything in the individual life must orbit God. We need a Copernican revolution. We need to see that in God's universe, planet earth is not the center. We are not the center. You are not the center. We need to go back to the Bible and see God for who He until His spiritual mass pulls every area of our life into His orbit.

Knowing God is costly. Don't fool yourself. If you want to know Him, you will have to lay all that you are, all that you plan to be, and all that you have on the table. If, at any moment, you pull it back, the process of getting to know God comes to a halt. There will be no progress. He will reveal Himself to His children, but He will not reveal Himself unless He has access, full access, to you. It is costly, but oh, it is worth it!

Although biblical Christianity is not all about us, nothing benefits us more. Nothing is more directly beneficial than knowing God. Nothing is more practical. Nothing is more relevant. Nothing is more exciting. Nothing is more satisfying than knowing the uncreated Being through His son.

The last of the four truths is a warning. If you are to know God as the believer longs to know God, you must, at all costs, avoid counterfeit versions of knowing God. There are ways of appearing to know God, which (like a counterfeit) from a distance seem to be a real knowing. They look genuine, and you may even get praised by people in your church. Despite these appearances, God knows that you don't know Him, and you know that you are not satisfied. Something is wrong.

There are three counterfeits [7] that I want to mention. The first is this: knowing God by hearsay.[8] This occurs when someone asks you a spiritual question, and you answer, "Well, my preacher says," or "I read in a book once," or "I remember my mother used to say…" Though it can be good to learn from other people, when it comes to knowing the one true God, don't you want something other than second-hand knowledge? Don't you want something other than hearsay? If you only know God by what you read in someone else's book, if you only know God by what you heard in someone else's sermon, then it is all second-hand. Someone else has pressed in; someone else has pressed on to know God. You may read or hear the results of another's pursuit of God and think you know God, but you don't. Second-hand knowledge—knowing God by hearsay—is not enough. If you are satisfied to know God by hearsay, it is the death of really knowing Him. You'll stop short.

The second counterfeit is textualism. Textualism[9] can be defined as mistaking an allegiance to a text for the possession of what the text teaches. For example, you own a Bible, and you're a conservative Christian. As a result, you say, "I give my allegiance to this book. And whatever is inside this book, I agree with it. Now, I'm not saying I know it. I haven't said I've studied it carefully. But if it's in this book, I'm for it." If a preacher or friend says, "In Ephesians 3, Paul talks about knowing the love of God—the length, the breadth, the height, the depth that is beyond knowledge—and being filled up with all the fullness of God that He might receive all the glory in the church in all ages," you can only respond, "Well, listen. I'm sorry. Maybe you didn't hear me. I believe this book. I don't remember Ephesians saying that. I haven't read Ephesians, but I told you I believe this book, and so whatever you quote from this book, I've already agreed with it." If you are satisfied with textualism, then it's the death of really knowing God.

The last counterfeit is the phenomenon of true truths.[10] This occurs when truths are so familiar to us, so obviously true, that instead of making an impact on our life, we shuffle them to a back cabinet in our mind and leave them there untouched. They no longer make any difference in the way we live. One example of a true truth is the fact that the earth is round. You know the earth is round, but it is not the kind of truth that made any difference to you this morning, is it? Did anyone disagree with the roundness of the earth? No. Waking up and knowing the earth is round didn't affect the way you dressed. When you looked into your closet, the roundness of the earth didn't really do anything for you. When you sat and ate breakfast this morning, you didn't eat in light of the roundness of the earth. You didn't drive your car in a certain way because the earth is round. You didn't choose the music you listen to or make choices about the way you spoke to your family based on the earth's roundness. It's a true truth. You are familiar with it. You don't think about it. It doesn't affect you.

If we're not careful, the great statements that we have heard over and over about God's character can become true truths that no longer affect us. Consider the truth that God is omnipresent. Any person who believes the Bible would agree that the Bible says that God fills the heavens and the earth. He fills the universe, and your hometown. That's where God lives. He's everywhere. He's everywhere at the same moment. Wherever I go today, God is there already. God is the environment that I have lived in every moment of my life, and He will be my environment forever and ever. I cannot lock a door and lock God out. I cannot turn out the lights and blind God. If I whisper, He will hear it. Every good deed and every bad deed, every sinful thought, is done right before the face of God. He's everywhere. Now, you would agree that God is omnipresent. Well, we say, "Yes, the Bible says it." But is it a true truth? Have you packed it away in the back cabinet of your mind so that it no longer makes a difference in the way you live? Did you choose your clothes this morning based on the reality that you are before the living God who is holy? Did the reality of God's omnipresence affect the way you ate today, the way you drove, spoke, worked? Did His nearness affect what you chose to watch or listen to or look at? If you want to truly know God, you must bring these "true truths" to the forefront of your mind, dust them off, and dwell on them until they alter your life.

Now, what do these counterfeits have in common? They are all cheap. They are versions of knowing God, a type of knowing God, that does not cost you anything. You do not have to lay it all on the table to say you agree with the Bible, to have hearsay knowledge of God, or to have a life unaffected by true truths.

Another thing these counterfeits have in common is this: they are respectable. Where are they most respectable? In the one place where they ought to be exposed, but they are not: the church. No one gets scolded for coming to church and saying, "I read a great book. You know what you said about God? I agree because I read Hudson Taylor, and Hudson Taylor said the same thing." And people think, "Wow. What a wonderful Christian you are. You read Hudson Taylor. You read so-and-so. You listen to sermons during the day. I wish I was that kind of Christian. I wish I knew God like that person knows Him." No one ever pulls you aside in church and says, "Do you know God? Or do you only know what other people say about God?" While counterfeit knowledge *looks* great, it is ineffective. It does not alter anything about our lives. It leaves us unsatisfied and disillusioned. Do you want to know God for yourself? To do so, we must expose the counterfeit and seek the real.

Remember Hosea's challenge on that dark day. "So let us know, let us press on to know the LORD. His going forth is as certain as the dawn; and He will come to us like the rain, like the spring rain watering the earth" (Hosea 6:3). Is Hosea telling the truth for our day? The answer cannot be given with your mouth. It can only be answered by what you do next. Will you put it to the test?

[1] John Bunyan and Alexander Philip, *The Practical Works of John Bunyan: With a Preliminary Essay on His Character and Writings, vol. 5* (United Kingdom: G. King, 1842), 198.
[2] A. W. Tozer, *The Pursuit of God* (Camp Hill, PA: Christian Publications, 1993), 19.
[3] A. W. Tozer, *The Knowledge of the Holy* (New York: Harper Collins Publishers, 1961), 1.
[4] Ibid
[5] Tozer, *The Knowledge of the Holy,* 2.
[6] Mark A. Noll, *America's God: From Jonathan Edwards to Abraham Lincoln* (United Kingdom: Oxford University Press, 2002), 191.
[7] Indebted to A. W. Tozer for thoughts on knowing God by hearsay, textualism, and true truths.
[8] A. W. Tozer, *The Deeper Life* (Grand Rapids: Zondervan, 1984), 64.
[9] Tozer, *The Deeper Life*, 3.
[10] Samuel Coleridge, *Aids to Reflection*, *Aphorism 1* (Liverpool: Edward Howell, 1873), 1.

The highest priority of our day must be a full return to the God of the entire Bible.

RICHARD OWEN ROBERTS

2

BEHOLDING GOD

Clearing the Way for Our Return

Is the God you know the God of the Bible? Descriptions of God in Scripture may not match the image of God in the modern mind. The ungodly king Nebuchadnezzar, after being dramatically humbled by God, described the Lord as follows: "I, Nebuchadnezzar, lifted my eyes to heaven, and my understanding returned to me; and I blessed the Most High and praised and honored Him who lives forever: for His dominion is an everlasting dominion and His kingdom is from generation to generation. All the inhabitants of the earth are reputed as nothing. He does according to His will in heaven and among the inhabitants of the earth. No one can restrain His hand or say to Him, 'What have You done?'" (Daniel 4:34–35). In Psalm 113, the psalmist writes, "Who is like the LORD our God, who dwells on high, who humbles Himself to behold the things in heaven and on earth?" David writes, "You are not a God who takes pleasure in wickedness. Nor shall evil dwell with You. The boastful shall not stand in Your sight. You hate all workers of iniquity" (Psalm 5:4–5). The prophet Nahum writes, "God is jealous, and the LORD avenges. The LORD avenges and is furious. The LORD will take vengeance on His adversaries, and He reserves wrath for His enemies" (Nahum 1:2). Do these passages describe the God whom you know? Do they tell of the God whom you long for? These are vital questions because these Scriptures reveal the only true God who exists.

The lives of many modern Christians are at odds with biblical descriptions of Christianity. In John 10:10, Christ says, "I have come that they may have life, and that they may have it more abundantly." In 1 Peter 1:7–8, the apostle writes, "Jesus... whom having not seen you love. Though you do not see Him, yet believing, you rejoice with joy inexpressible and full of glory." In Colossians 1:9–12, Paul records an astonishing prayer for the young church: "We do not cease to pray for you and ask that you may be filled with the knowledge of His will in all wisdom and spiritual understanding that you may walk worthy of the Lord, fully pleasing Him, being fruitful in every good work and increasing in the knowledge of God, strengthened with all might, according to His glorious power for all patience and long suffering with joy." Is your Christianity like this? Is this the life you long for, living solely for the glory of your King?

The contrast between our lives and these verses reveals a significant departure from legitimate biblical experience. The contrast is inextricably tied to our drift from the biblical God. We may not recognize the danger we are in because we have been adrift for so long that we begin to view our condition as normal Christianity. We become accustomed to the enormous gap between our lives and biblical Christianity. If we ever become alarmed, those around us say that we need to accept today's standards. Maybe we will be told to work harder in the church and then things will be okay. Surface level adjustments will not make things okay. And we cannot pretend that they are okay because God's Word will continue to convict and convince us that root level change is needed.

As we read the Bible, we become aware that there is a gap

between what we are living and what we are reading. This gap plagues us. We look at our departure from the Lord, and we see that the way back is a long road filled with briars and thorns. The briars and thorns are our sins and their effects. Every day that we drift from the biblical view of God, every day that we live for ourselves, we pile new barriers behind us. When Scripture convicts us, we want to turn and go back, but we see the length of the road and the briars in the way, and we think, "I don't know if I *can* return."

The time may come when you want to return, and you struggle to believe it is possible. You may think there is no way for you to know the biblical God, the abundant life, the joy inexpressible and full of glory—no way for you to walk worthy of the Lord, fully pleasing Him. For most of us, this kind of life, though admirable and desirable, seems unattainable. But put your doubts aside. Rejoice! Through Christ, it is not only possible to know Him in this way, it is also the birthright of every believer.

If we are to have the joy inexpressible of knowing Him, we must be honest about a few difficult truths. Returning to God requires that we turn away from the sins and idols that have charmed us. We must stop believing the lies which have taken the place of truth. There are three important truths that we need to believe and apply if we are going to remove the thorns and briars and clear the way for our return.

The first truth is this: a correct diagnosis of our spiritual problem is essential to an effective and lasting cure. An accurate diagnosis is always important. If you take your car to a garage and hand it over to a mechanic, he will diagnose the problem and tell you what is involved in the repair. You must go through the inconvenience of losing your car for a few days and the inconvenience of paying the mechanic. But what if you get the car back and the problem is still there? Now, maybe the mechanic fixed another problem, but he didn't fix the problem you were concerned about. Frustration, delay, and expense are all a result of the misdiagnosis. In a more sobering situation, if you go to a doctor, and he misdiagnoses a very deadly disease, there is much more at stake than a frustrating delay, isn't there? A misdiagnosis from a doctor could cost you your life. But there is a more critical situation than these: a spiritual misdiagnosis may endanger your eternal soul.

A wrong diagnosis will always lead us to an inadequate cure. We may treat the symptoms instead of the root problem. How do we treat symptoms in our modern era? Many people look out of the windows of the church, so to speak, and say, "You know what we need? We need to find a way to get those people out there attracted to what we're doing in here. The problem in our day is that we need to get prayer back in school. We need different politicians. We need to send out more missionaries. We need to collect more money."

Perhaps more insightful Christians look within the church and say, "No, the problem is that people inside the church are indifferent and apathetic. They've grown cold and materialistic. They are joyless and purposeless. Dads aren't the spiritual leaders they ought to be. Our marriages are in peril." Now, these are all serious problems, and it is important to address them, but none are the primary problem. It is easy to misdiagnose the situation and think that these are the issues that ought to absorb our time.

We get busy treating symptoms. We buy Christian books; we write Christian books. We watch Christian movies; we make Christian movies. Christian jewelry is sold with little messages on it. Twenty years down the line, are we really a people concerned about "What would Jesus do?" after owning so many "WWJD" bracelets? Twenty years after *The Purpose Driven Life*, do we go to church and see a people full of a sense of their true purpose? Or do they look like everyone else around them—purposeless, empty, confused? Do we find radical Christians occupying the pews because they read the book *Radical*? Will we find fireproof marriages? Will we find families led by spiritually courageous dads? It's very easy to waste years of earnest, sincere effort as a believer because we misdiagnose the problem.

Objections might be raised. Finding a purpose in life, strengthening a marriage, getting a dad spiritually involved—certainly these are good. But if you think these symptoms are the great problems, then you are in danger. What is the danger? Good efforts can worsen the problem if rooted in a misdiagnosis.

Imagine a sick person going to the doctor, and the doctor — without doing a thorough investigation of the problem—says, "Well, I think the problem is that you need more exercise, a healthier diet, and better sleep." Those are all good suggestions. But what if there is a hidden cancer? Then a misdiagnosis causes precious time to be wasted. A disease that might have been curable now becomes a disease that is fatal. It is the same in the spiritual realm. A spiritual misdiagnosis wastes precious time. A misdiagnosis leads to problems in the church becoming fatal problems because only the symptoms are being treated, not the root problem.

What is the problem? The problem is not the culture around us. It is not the new atheism. It is not secularism. It is not humanism. It is not materialism. The root issue is this: Christians have embraced a light God, and they have propagated this light version of God. The preacher's words are weightless because his God is weightless. When the church gives its witness to the world, our words are weightless—they are empty words because our God is weightless. It is not that we are not relevant enough to the culture. It is that we have forgotten to be relevant to God Himself. We are plenty relevant to the culture. We understand the culture. We fit right in with the culture. The culture even feels at home with us. But the important question is this: Does God feel at home with us?

Our problem within the church is that we are suffering a thousand consequences of embracing a low and inadequate view of God.

In Psalm 50, God describes this precise situation. He gives a list of sins that grieve Him. The people He is speaking to are still religious. They are still going to the temple and offering sacrifices. They are still saying their prayers. They are still singing their religious songs. But God is grieved, and He gives the diagnosis: "You thought I was altogether like you" (Psalm 50:21).

This is the only way to explain so much of what goes on in the modern church. The only way to explain acting the way we act, saying the things we say, doing the things we do, leaving undone the things that we leave undone—is that we think God is like us. Believing that God is like us is the undiagnosed cancer of evangelicalism.

The good news is that we only have one problem to deal with, and we only have one Person to satisfy. We can't fix Hollywood. We can't fix atheistic universities. We can't even fix the people who live under our own roof. What can we do? We can turn our hearts back to the biblical descriptions of God. We can put things right vertically. Our return to the biblical view of God does not mean that every problem disappears and life becomes easy. It does, however, mean the internal problems and external problems the church is facing take on a proper perspective when God Himself is central.

The second truth is that there are connections between certain beliefs. You can read the Bible earnestly and miss much benefit if you don't understand this. There are unbreakable connections. The first important belief is what you believe about God. What you believe about God affects number two, which is what you believe about self. What you believe about God and self affects number three, what you believe about sin. Those three affect number four, what you believe about salvation.[1]

Are you a person who by carelessness embraces a low and unbiblical view of God? It is possible to be faithful to church and Christian moral values and embrace a god of your imagination. But be aware, a small view of God always produces an inflated view of yourself. It is impossible to avoid this connection. If you allow small and contemporary views of God to fill the heart, then a large and inflated view of self is the product. And if you have a small view of God and a large view of yourself, it will necessarily give you a warped view of sin.

When you have a small view of God, you believe sin is terrible only because it affects you. Your life, your happiness is the center of your existence. This wrong view makes sin's biggest problem the fact that sin will make you unhappy and lead you to hell. If you have a small view of God, a large view of self, and a wrong view of sin, then you will have a wrong view of salvation. You will think that salvation is primarily about you avoiding the negative consequences of sin. You are promised heaven instead of hell, you are given peace at night instead of a troubled conscience, and you gain a friend who will never leave you. God takes your life, He cleans it, He polishes it, He promises you a happy destination, and He hands it back to you. You are still in charge, and you are still the center.

Now imagine a person who is very careful to cultivate a high view of God. This high view of God naturally causes the view of self to shrink and to take the right proportion. God is the center, not self. When God is the center, then sin is seen accurately. Sin is not just a thing that will bring negative consequences into your life. Sin is a thief, a thief of God's glory. The glory God rightly deserves from you is stolen by the sin your heart is embracing. Now when you understand these realities, salvation becomes a much greater thing. Salvation is not merely promising you heaven and a friend who will never leave; instead, salvation is dealing with the totality of sin. Salvation now means your heart is transformed, your mind is enlightened, and your will is free. You choose Christ. You want what is clean. You believe and submit to what God says. This wonderful change results in a fundamentally different life. You are not perfect, but you are different. The process has begun by which your sin will ultimately be brought under the feet of Christ. Salvation means each day, you have the opportunity, by the grace of God, to give Him the glory you now want to give Him. The great thing about salvation is that He is going to be glorified! This tremendous change is cultivated when biblical truths are approached in a correct order: God, self, sin, and salvation.

A correct diagnosis and a recognition of the order and connections of biblical truths leads us to the third truth. In order to clear the briars and open the road back to God, root sins must be distinguished from fruit sins, and both require repentance. What are root and fruit sins? How do we differentiate between the two? Fruit sins are sins that are obvious and exist on the surface of life. They are the ugly sins other people see. They are the sins that embarrass us as individuals. They embarrass us as families. They embarrass us as churches. It does no lasting good to repent of only the fruit sins while leaving the root sins untouched. Imagine a man who wants a perfect yard, but dandelions have overtaken his yard. Every Saturday morning, he gets up early and works in his yard. He takes a pair of scissors and he carefully manicures his lawn by chopping off all the dandelion heads. When he is done, his yard looks immaculate. But, by the end of the week, his yard doesn't look so perfect. He has even more dandelions everywhere! He brings out the scissors, and another Saturday is spent chopping off dandelion heads. At the end of the day, he looks at his yard and says, "It's good again." But he'll have to repeat it, won't he? Over and over and over, every week, because he hasn't dealt with the roots.

What are root sins? Root sins are the sins lurking under the surface of life. They are hidden and hard to detect. All other sins grow from these breeder sins. The root sins revealed to us through Scripture are the sins of pride, unbelief, and selfishness. Root sins can be seen in the following illustration. A man was caught in adultery.

When this man first came to his pastor, he was very contrite. He confessed how sorry he was and how terrible he knew his actions were. But when the pastor really pressed him about the seriousness of his sin, he became angry, and said, “You don’t know the woman I live with!” His outburst revealed that he felt justified in his sin. But why? Do you see the problem? He was willing enough to admit the fruit sin was wrong, “I shouldn’t have committed adultery.” But he did not acknowledge or repent of the root sins. The sin of pride — “I have a right to act this way.” The sin of unbelief: “I don’t believe what God and the Bible say about my actions.” The sin of selfishness: “I have a right to have what I want.” All of these root sins were untouched. Until he acknowledges and repents of the root sins, his fruit sins will only be repeated later, like dandelions rearing their ugly heads.

No root sin can thrive in a life that is, by God’s grace, pursuing an ever-clearer view of God. How can a man be proud when he is aware of the majesty of God? How can he be unbelieving when he sees the faithfulness of God? How can he be selfish when he is constantly brought into contact with the goodness of God? Until we are willing to see God as He is and repent of our root sins, we will never really clear away the briars. We will never really go back to God.

Can we afford it? Can we afford to go on as we have, drifting along with a false view of God, building briar barriers on the road to Him? Can your children afford for you to waste ten more years misdiagnosing the problem at home? Can the church members afford for their pastors to spend ten more years dealing with fruit sins but leaving the roots untouched? Can the world around us afford ten more years of the church focusing on secondary issues and failing to return to the Lord? We must not wait a moment; we must wrestle now with these three truths and apply them in our lives. We must set our faces to return to God, whatever the cost.

[1] Richard Owen Roberts, *Salvation in Full Color* (Wheaton: International Awakening Press, 1994), xii.

As we treat the Word of God, so should we treat God Himself, were He to come and reside among us in a human form, as He once dwelt on earth in the form of His Son.

EDWARD PAYSON

3

BEHOLDING GOD

The Bible

In his book, *The Divine Conquest,* A. W. Tozer writes, "We have as much of God as we actually want."[1] This is a troubling comment for believers because it gets behind our Christian masks and exposes the real us. Is it true that in Christ we have as much of God as we want? You may ask, "How well can a person really know God? How close can a Christian walk to God?" The answer is that no believer has ever reached the bottom of that great well because it has no bottom. No limit can exist in God's nature. There is always more of Him to know.

Let's examine two attributes that illustrate God's limitlessness: His infinity and His immutability.

God is infinite. He is without limit. Because He is infinite, every other attribute—everything that God reveals about Himself, every truth about His character—is without limit and without measure. He is love, holy, just, eternal, all-knowing, all-powerful, and all-present. Each of these aspects of God's character is limitless. Because every attribute of God is without limit, we cannot fully understand Him.

While we can know many true things about God, and we can know all that we need for godliness in this life, none of us will ever get our minds around the greatness of God. Edward Payson (1783-1827), an American pastor, wrote, "God, how much this one word implies. No human or angelic tongue can ever express, no mind can conceive. He is a book made up of infinite number of pages. Every page is full of meaning. It will be studied by saints and angels through all the ages and into eternity, but they will never reach the last page, nor will they ever comprehend the meaning of even a single page."[2] God incomprehensible. Payson used this illustration: "I would ask you to pause and contemplate, for a moment, this wonderful Being. But where shall we stand to take a view of Him? When we wish to contemplate the ocean, we take our stand upon its shore. But this infinite ocean of being and perfection has no shore. There is no place where we can stand to look at Him, for He is in us, around us, above us, below us. Yet, in another sense, there is no place where we may not look at Him, for He is everywhere. We see nothing which He has not made, no motion which He does not cause; for He is all, and in all, and above all, God over all, blessed forever."[3]

God is not only infinite and without measure; He is also immutable. This attribute should inform all of our thoughts about Him. Timothy Dwight, another early American pastor, wrote, "[God] is subject to no change in His manner of being, His perfections, thoughts, desires, purposes, or determinations."[4] He is incapable of change. God cannot increase, we know. He cannot diminish. He is incapable of being shifted or altered from without." When we open the Scripture to know God, we are seeking the only God who does not—who cannot, by His own decree—change. The God who called all matter into existence is the God whom you are called to know. The God who sought out Abram is the God whom you are called to know. The God who walked with Enoch, the God who taught Moses, the God who gave the shepherd boy, David, songs in the night is the God whom you are called to know. There is no difference between the God of the Old Testament and the God of the New Testament. The joy of the believer is this: that the one infinite, boundless Being who cannot change is the one Being whom we must know.

Striving to know a limitless, immutable God requires the right tools, used in the right way. In the midst of the Great Awakening, John Wesley looked at his Methodists and was concerned they were becoming lazy. He accused them of "religious enthusiasm," which is equivalent to religious fanaticism. He warned them against this fanaticism in which people claim to have a desire to know God but neglect the means God placed in their hands for that purpose. Are we guilty of this as well? We talk about knowing God, wanting to know Him better, and wanting to walk closer to Him; but are we neglecting the very means God gave us for this purpose?

What tools has God provided so that we may know Him? The single most significant tool is the Bible. Most of us own a Bible. Most of us actually own several Bibles, so the problem isn't that we lack this tool; it is that we neglect or misuse Scripture. You may neglect to study the Bibles that you own—the Bibles so easily accessible in your home, even on the phone in your hand. You may say you are too busy for careful and earnest study of the Scriptures—Scriptures which are given and inspired by the immutable, infinite God of creation. Yet, you are not too busy for other things.

Along with this inexcusable neglect, misuse of the Bible is a common problem. Throughout history, some people have studied the Scriptures diligently, but at the end of a lifetime of study, they have not known God. One of the most notorious examples of this is the Pharisee. A New Testament Pharisee would have memorized every word of the first five books of the Old Testament. Every Pharisee did. The Pharisee worked a normal job and spent his evenings in religious study. The Pharisee was the pinnacle of spirituality. After all this work and study, the Pharisees were still so little acquainted with the God of the Bible that when God came in the Person of His Son, Immanuel, they did not even recognize Him. Instead, they demanded His death. How could scholars of this magnitude be so far from the truth of God? It is because they misused the Bible.

How do we avoid the failure of the Pharisees? Is there a scientific method for avoiding these mistakes? Are there four or five key questions you ought to ask in coming to every text: who, what, when, where, and why? Is understanding Greek and Hebrew the key? Perhaps purchasing a new study Bible will guarantee that you will never be like the Pharisees. While study Bibles, commentaries, concordances, and proper techniques for interpreting the text are all helpful, it is necessary to back up to see the bigger picture. How does rethinking our view of God change the way we approach the Bible?

The first significant question to ask in approaching the Bible is this: Who is this book about? Now, that seems like a question with an obvious answer—a Sunday school answer—but it is not so simple. When we read the stories of Moses, David, Daniel, and the prophets, we may think that the Bible is simply an account of spiritual heroes. For example, Sunday school material on the book of Daniel often focuses on the life of Daniel and forgets the God of Daniel. Focusing solely on the life of the man Daniel, the application of the book of Daniel is how to excel in an irreligious environment. Daniel is the example and hero. But that is not primarily what the book of Daniel is about. In one Sunday school curriculum, the truth that the teacher was directed to emphasize regarding the account of Noah and the ark was this: God cares for animals. Well, that is astonishing since it is the one time in history when God killed all the animals except for two of each kind.

Maybe you don't think Noah or Daniel are the heroes; instead, you think Scripture is all about *you*. Specialized Bibles are one indication of this growing trend. There are Bibles that relate to certain ages such as the teen Bible or the retired person's Bible. There are gender-specific Bibles. There are Bibles for people with certain hobbies: the hunter's Bible and the athlete's Bible. Within these, you will find devotionals or comments written by people like you for people like you. If you're an athlete, an athlete will give you a thought for the day suited to an athlete. The focus is you and your needs, not God. The American religious industry knows if they can make a Bible that suits you personally, you will buy it. This points to a root problem: we think the Bible is first and foremost about *us*.

Wrong approaches to Scripture are not limited to Christian publishers. We often open the Bible for our daily quiet time and proceed to adapt the Bible to fit us. We treat it like a medicine cabinet. We open the Bible and pick a pill for the day that will encourage, comfort, or strengthen us. Of course, God's Word does provide encouragement, comfort, and strength for the believer. But the Bible should not be approached as a medicine cabinet where we choose a verse to help us with a specific spiritual problem in the same way we would choose a pill to help us with a physical problem.

Think of it this way: We often the use the Bible like wrapping paper. We take the pages out of the Bible and sew them together and create a great wrap that we bend around our life. While those pages have the same words, same concepts, and the same truths, it is now bent around an entirely different object. It is no longer a series of statements primarily about God. Instead, we have made it a series of statements primarily about us, what we want, and what we need—totally focused on ourselves. Do you see our need to rethink how we approach the Bible?

If this is the greatest tool God has given you to know Him, isn't a right use of that tool of immense consequence? When we rethink our approach to the Bible, we must begin by asking: Who is the Bible really about? The Bible is a book about God. He is the key actor in each scene. This truth, which may seem simplistic, has a significant effect when it is applied.

The second question is: What is the purpose of this book? If we are going to rethink God and approach Scripture differently, we are going to have to ask this question: What is the purpose of the Bible? The Bible is helpful in so many ways that you may lose the primary purpose amid all the secondary benefits. It is critically important to discern between the primary and secondary purposes of Scripture. There is one primary purpose and there are many secondary purposes. When we say secondary, we do not mean unimportant; the Bible speaks about several topics that touch our lives and are of great importance. We use the term secondary in the sense that these purposes do not stand alone. For instance, we read the Bible to know how to raise our children but explaining how to raise children is not the primary purpose of the Bible. The Bible is primarily about God. And as God is unveiled, it becomes clear that we ought to raise our children in a certain way because of who God is.

What is the primary purpose of the Bible? First, it is important to clarify what is not its primary purpose. The primary purpose of the Bible is not dictated by your present crisis. We all go through difficult times and when we have a crisis, we really want to come to God and ask, "What does this book say about my problem?" The purpose of the Bible rises above our felt needs.

The Bible is not, as we have heard it described, primarily an owner's manual for life. It is frequently treated this way. What do we do with owner's manuals? If we buy a gadget and don't understand how it works, we get out our owner's manual. We read the manual until we understand, and then we put it away. Unless we have a problem, the manual is of no use to us.

How many people come to a church, hear a sermon, and say to the preacher, "I want to be a Christian. I don't want to go to hell. I don't want to be alone. I don't want my conscience to be constantly plagued." The preacher responds, "Great! Christ will enter your life. Here's the book for you. Read it." These people take their Bibles home. At first, they are hungry to know something about God, something about themselves, and something about the Christian life. After a while, they figure that they've really got it under their belt, and they take their "owner's manual" and put it in a drawer. When things become difficult, they run back to the drawer and pull out their Bible and ask God to please fix their problems.

The Bible is not an owner's manual for life. The Bible is very unsuitable as an owner's manual, even though it says so much about life. Think about the way God has arranged the material in the Bible. Which book of the Bible is called "The Book of Family"? But family is important! Which book of the Bible is called "The Book of Marriage"? Is there even a book called "The Book of How to Do Church"? Which chapter of the Bible is on money? Which chapter is on career choice? Which chapter describes retirement?

The Bible is perfectly designed for one purpose above all others. The Bible unveils a Person—a Person who is so unlike anyone we have ever met that the only way for us to really know Him is through the book He has given us. This book, the Bible, reveals Him through various types of literature: history, law, songs, prayers, proverbs, sermons, and prophecies. All these types of literature are skillfully crafted to show us God from different angles. That is the purpose of the Bible—to reveal God. What method should we use to approach such a book?

The method used must be based on the primary purpose of the tool. We should read the Bible to get to know God. When we open our Bibles in our quiet times or when we attend church and the pastor reads the text, there ought to be an earnest longing: "God, what do we learn of You in this passage? Why do You reveal Yourself in this way? Why do You say this about Yourself to this people in this situation? What does that teach me about You?"

Now in some passages, the answer to that question is obvious because God is distinctly described by Himself or by divinely inspired people. These passages are clear-cut and straightforward. Other passages require us to stop and think awhile. "How do I see God in this passage?" It is important to keep every passage in its context as we see God revealed in Scripture. God progressively unveils Himself from Genesis to Revelation. Every passage does not overtly describe God and His divine nature, but every passage is part of the flow of God's unveiling of Himself.

One example of Scripture that is more difficult to see as God-centered is the Ten Commandments. This set of commandments might seem to be about us. When we read the Ten Commandments we think, "This is about our behavior. It's not about God. God doesn't need ten commandments to stay in line." No, He doesn't. So, how do we see God as the primary focus of the Ten Commandments?

To approach the passage properly, remembering that God's self-revelation is the primary purpose, we should first examine its context. The Ten Commandments didn't just appear. These commandments were given to a particular people in a specific situation at a certain place and time. The Israelites had been in Egypt for nearly four hundred years. Most of them had no understanding of what their God was like. They only understood Egyptian idolatry. Once they were brought out of Egyptian slavery and rescued from the Egyptian army, the next thing God did was rescue them from Egyptian ideas of gods by teaching them about His character—the character of the one true God. Through a series of miracles, disciplines, and the gift of Scripture, God begins to reveal His unique nature to them. He reveals that He is not like any of the Egyptian gods in any way. He gives them the Ten Commandments which are an unveiling of His moral perfection. Unlike the corrupt, immoral Egyptian gods, the living God delights in purity, holiness, and righteousness. So, even the Ten Commandments ultimately reveal something that we need to know about God.

If you are going to walk with a God like this, then He wants you to delight in the same things He does—purity, holiness, and righteousness. If you are going to reflect a God like Him to others who are clueless about Him, then you are going to have to live according to His values.

Rethinking God will change our approach to Scripture, which should change our idea of salvation. A popular but unbiblical thought about salvation is that conversion is everything. When truly converted, I come to God in faith and repentance, I receive the great promises, and I hand my life over to Him. Through Christ's great work for me, I am His, and He is mine. But when we begin to rethink God, we realize that conversion is not the end. It is not the end of coming to the Bible to know Him. It is only the beginning.

There is never, in fact, an end to the right use of Scripture in this life. There is never a retirement age. There is never a time when we can stop pursuing Him. Before we came to God in Christ, we lived in the dungeon of spiritual death. It was dark. It was restricted and narrow—a prison cell. The only pleasures we had were the pleasures that can be had in a filthy dungeon. Christ comes, breaks the lock, and through His life and death rescues us; we walk out of the underground dungeon up into the light to breathe the clean air. Before us, we can imagine a Switzerland-like place. There are mountains, lakes, valleys, fields, and streams. God calls us to explore it all. "Well," we say, "It's wonderful. The only thing that makes me sad is the thought that one day I will wake up and say, 'Well, I've explored it all.'" "No," God says, "There are no boundaries to this land. I want you, not only in this life, but in eternity, to explore and explore and explore who I am." God Himself will be our travelling companion. And God Himself will be our guide. The Spirit of Christ takes us, and with the Scripture, we begin the great adventure of knowing God—an adventure that never ends.

One passage that illustrates what it means to rethink God and how rethinking God affects the way we approach Scripture is found in the book of Job, chapters 38–42. Who is this man, Job? God describes him as a righteous man, an upright man, a man who fears God, and a man who turns from evil.[5] Job is an older man with adult children. He is respected by his community, but there is a problem. It is not a problem of suffering. There is suffering, but the book of Job is not primarily about suffering. The book of Job is not primarily about patience. The book of Job is about Job's God.

Throughout the various hardships Job experiences, he complains and questions a great deal. His friends give him misguided counsel. Job knows God, Job believes God, Job obeys God, and Job loves God. He has the right categories for God in his mind: God is all-present; God is all knowing; God is all-powerful; God is eternal; God is holy. The real problem with Job is that each category is too small. God draws Job aside and exposes His greatness to him. He pulls back the veil. Job's small view of God is exploded—expanded. Through divine revelation, Job's view of God is greatly enlarged.

Although Job knows God, he still has so much to learn. He is on a road; and on that road, he has travelled a long way. Yet, because the road of knowing God is endless, Job still has an infinite distance to travel. There's so much more of God to know. To bring him further along that road, God teaches Job a lesson. In Job 38:2–3, God takes Job aside and tells him, "Who is this that darkens counsel by words without knowledge? Now prepare yourself like a man; and I will question you, and you will answer me!" or to paraphrase, "Job, you have said a lot of things and you think you know a lot. Who are you to question My wisdom? Now get ready. I have some questions for you. Since you know so much, you can teach Me." Job is given two rounds of questions. They are strange questions to us, but they all have the same purpose. The purpose is for Job to see God elevated. Job must feel that the distance between him and God is much greater than he has ever understood it to be.

Here are some of God's questions to Job. "Where were you when I laid the foundations of the earth? Tell Me, if you have understanding. Who determined its measurements? Surely you know" (Job 38:4). In other words, He is saying, "Job, you've been doing a lot of talking. Let Me ask you, where were you when I measured out the earth? You, of all men, should know." Job doesn't know. As the chapter proceeds, God asks, "Have you commanded the morning since your days began? Have you entered the springs of the sea? Tell Me, if you know all of this! Where is the way to the dwelling of light? Can you lift your voice to the clouds that an abundance of water may cover you? Can you send out lightnings that they may go and say, 'Here we are'? Who has put wisdom in the mind?" (Job 38: 12, 16, 18, 19, 34–36). The questions just keep coming. In Job 40:4, Job responds to the Lord, "Behold, I am vile; what shall I answer You? I lay my hand over my mouth. Once I have spoken, but I will not answer; yes, twice, but I will proceed no further."

As God reveals Himself and His nature to Job, Job begins to feel that he has no right to open his mouth. Yes, Job has talked before—but now his hand goes over his mouth. Yet this response is not good enough. The problem goes deeper than that. Even though Job is ready for the surgery to be over, God knows there is still work to be done, so He takes Job through the questioning process again. In chapter 40, He asks even more penetrating questions. "Have you an arm like God? Can you thunder with a voice like His? Then adorn yourself with majesty and splendor and array yourself with glory and beauty. Disperse the rage of your wrath and look on everyone who is proud and humble them" (Job 40:9–11). Is that you, Job? A significant man on planet earth, a godly man, an impressive man, a man who's looked up to. Job, do you have an arm like God's? Do you have a voice like God's? Can you look at one arrogant person—one self-sufficient man—humble him, and make him feel his need for God? No, you cannot. If you could do this, "then I will confess to you that your own right hand could save you" (Job 40:14).

The questions continue, and God compares Job to the mighty animals He created. In essence God says to Job, "Job, you think you are like Me. You think that the gap is small, but I tell you, Job, that you are nothing. You are not even great enough to be compared to some of these animals that I made."[6]

When the questions stop, we find the effect of Job's fresh vision of God. In Job 42:2–6, Job responds to the Lord, "I know that You can do everything, and that no purpose of Yours can be withheld from You. You asked, 'Who is this who hides counsel without knowledge?' Therefore I have uttered what I did not understand, things too wonderful for me, which I did not know. Listen, please, and let me speak. You said, 'I will question you, and you shall answer Me.' I have heard of You by the hearing of the ear, but now my eyes see You. Therefore, I abhor myself, and I repent in dust and ashes."

This is a wonderful picture of what occurs every time we open the Scriptures and see God. While we are thankful for what we knew before, it is completely inadequate. As we know Him more, in a new way, we think, "Oh, God, it is like we can truly see You." Our new view of God gives us a new understanding of ourselves, and we find ourselves acknowledging, "I am nothing." This is one great test of whether you are approaching the Scriptures correctly: does God shock you? Does seeing God make you feel mighty small, and is it your delight to be small as you look upon Him?

Can you be trusted with a book that unveils God? A spiritual Copernican revolution is needed, and it begins with the Bible. It does not begin in our imagination, and it does not begin by us scurrying about trying to do great things for God. Spiritual revolution begins with Scripture. True spiritual revolution will cost us. It cost Abram everything. It cost Paul everything. It has cost Christians everything throughout history.

It cost the monk, Martin Luther, everything in the fifteen hundreds. Luther studied the Scriptures, and he came to the realization of who God is and how a person could truly be made right with Him. One biographer commented, "Luther's greatness is that he asked the right questions of the Scripture, and he was given, therefore, the right answers."[7] So, I want to ask you: Can you be trusted with this book? Will you ask the right questions? Will you open your Bible tomorrow in your quiet time and forget yourself? Be preoccupied with God? Do you have enough courage to say, "God, who are You? Show me." Do you have the courage to stay when the answers start coming, and they go against everything you once thought you knew?

Where are you intending to stop in the pursuit of knowing God? Have you, in fact, stopped already? Do you feel you have arrived? "Well," you say, "no." Maybe you intend to read the Bible until you get all the basic facts clear. Maybe you intend to read it until you're 65, maybe 70. Maybe you'll read it until people praise you because you are a knowledgeable Christian and an excellent Sunday school teacher. Remember, Job was praised by God and by people, but that was no place for him to stop. There is no stopping place on planet earth for the believer. We press on—press on to know the Lord. We do not stop using the Bible to know God until we see Christ face-to-face.

A. W. Tozer, in his book, *The Pursuit of God*, warned his Bible-reading church members: "It is not mere words that nourish the soul, but God Himself, and unless and until the hearers find God in personal experience they are not the better for having heard the truth." [8] The Bible is not an end, but a means to bring men to an intimate and satisfying knowledge of God. Rethinking God will cause a man, woman, or young person to completely rethink how he or she approaches the Scriptures. Are you willing to rethink your use of Scripture because of who He is? Do you want more of Him? Remember, believer, you may have as much of God as you actually want.

[1] A. W. Tozer, *The Divine Conquest* (New Jersey: Fleming H. Revell Co., 1950), 122.
[2] Edward Payson, *Memoir, Select Thoughts and Sermons of the Late Rev. Edward Payson, Pastor of the Second Church in Portland* (Philadelphia: Hyde, Lord & Duren, 1846), 1:459.
[3] Ibid
[4] Sereno Edwards Dwight and Timothy Dwight, *Theology Explained and Defended, Sermons; with a Memoir of the Life of the Author* (United Kingdom: np, 1819), 81.
[5] Job 1:1
[6] Author's summary of Job 41
[7] James Atkinson, *Martin Luther and the Birth of Protestantism* (1968; repr., Atlanta: John Knox Press, 1981), 49.
[8] A. W, Tozer, *The Pursuit of God* (Camp Hill, PA: Christian Publications, 1993), 9.

He that would find God must seek Him in Christ Jesus.

DANIEL DE SUPERVILLE

4

BEHOLDING GOD

The Face of Jesus Christ

God reveals Himself to us throughout Scripture, but He does so most clearly in the passages about Jesus. Some passages use shadowy types, symbols, ceremonies, and prophecies to speak of Christ. The Old Testament is full of these, and it is a great source for clues and hints about the coming God-man. In these prophesies, we can behold our God as we read about the Messiah. In the New Testament, the views are even clearer. There, the most brilliant and clear displays of God's perfection are seen in the life and labors of Jesus. One Puritan called this "noon-day divinity."[1] If you desire to remove those dark and cloudy spots that inhibit your view of God, the quickest way is to look at Him as He is reflected in His Son.

As we read church history, we find that in seasons of spiritual vitality, the church is focused on Christ. Whenever and wherever you find a healthy church, you will inevitably find that it is Christ-centered. It is Christ-centered in its teaching, singing, praying, giving, fellowshipping, and serving. It is even Christ-centered in its evangelism. When we find a healthy church, we always find an overriding preoccupation with Christ.

Examples of this preoccupation with Christ can be found throughout Scripture. The Messianic psalms contain several examples. Psalm 45 was written to celebrate the marriage of Solomon, yet the same passage appears again in the New Testament with reference to Christ (Hebrews 1:8–9). There is a dual application. In Psalm 45, we see a figure—a Davidic king—who is the small person in the forefront of the passage. Behind the son of David (Solomon) is the greater Son of David (Jesus) who is seen in the distance. Many descriptions of the king are too glorious to be about Solomon. For example, when this psalm praises the king with these words: "You are fairer than the sons of men" (Psalm 45:2), the writer is speaking not of Solomon, but of Christ. When we study these Messianic psalms, it is easy to see why the writers delighted to sing of Jesus.

Other examples of this fascination with Jesus are found in the Old Testament prophets. In Isaiah, we have passages that foretell the coming of Christ. In Isaiah 9:6–7, Isaiah writes, "Unto us a Child is born, unto us a Son is given; and the government will be upon His shoulder. And His name will be called Wonderful, Counselor, Mighty God, Everlasting Father, Prince of Peace. Of the increase of His government and peace there will be no end." The prophets waited expectantly for the Messiah who already captivated their hearts and minds.

Of course, in the New Testament, we find numerous expressions of Christ-centeredness. Peter and Paul both exemplify a preoccupation with Christ. Peter says of Jesus, "Whom having not seen you love. Though now you do not see Him, yet, believing, you rejoice with joy inexpressible and full of glory." Peter continues in the next chapter: "Therefore, to you who believe, He is precious" (1 Peter 1:8; 2:7).

Paul gives us autobiographical statements along the same line. In Galatians 2:20, he writes, "I have been crucified with Christ; it is no longer I who live, but Christ lives in me; and the life which I now live in the flesh I live by faith in the Son of God, who loved me and gave Himself for me." In Philippians 1:21, he tells us, "For to me, to live is Christ, and to die is gain." When Paul writes to the new church plant in the city of Colossae, he applies the same kind of thinking: "If then you were raised with Christ, seek those things which are above, where Christ is, sitting at the right hand of God. Set your mind on things above, not on things on the earth. For you died, and your life is hidden with Christ in God... Christ... is our life" (Colossians 3:1–4).

In addition to biblical examples of preoccupation with Christ, we have more than nineteen hundred years of testimony from men and women throughout church history who were also captivated with Him. Saint Ignatius was an early church leader in the second century who wrote, "Apart from Christ, let nothing dazzle you." In the second century, Bernard of Clairvaux wrote a hymn we often sing. One stanza says,

Jesus, Thou joy of loving hearts,

Thou fount of life, Thou light of men,

From the best bliss that earth imparts,

We turn unfilled to Thee again.

Later in the hymn, he writes,

To them that seek Thee Thou art good,

To them that find Thee, all in all.

In the seventeenth century, an English pastor named Isaac Ambrose wrote, "Nations, and all nations; gold, and all gold; jewels, and all jewels; angels, and all angels: all these, and every all besides all these; what are they in comparison of Christ, but as feathers, dung, shadows, nothing?"[2] In the nineteenth century, Frederick Faber—a hymnist known for his hymns about Christ—wrote, "Wherever we turn in the church of God there is Jesus. He is the beginning, the middle, and the end of everything for us . . . There is nothing good, nothing holy, nothing beautiful, nothing joyous, which He is not to His servants. We can exaggerate about many things, but we can never exaggerate about our obligation to Jesus or the compassionate abundance of the love of Jesus to us."[3] The Baptist pastor, Charles Spurgeon, wrote, "I'd rather be blind, deaf, and dumb, and lose my ability to taste and to smell than not to love Christ. To be unable to appreciate Christ is the worst of disabilities. It is the death of a soul." He warned the thousands who came to hear him, "If you cannot say, 'Jesus is precious to me,' I do not care to what church you belong or what creed you are ready to die for, you do not know the truth of God, unless the Person of Christ is dear to you." The very last words spoken by Charles Spurgeon after forty years of ministry were, "Christ is the most magnanimous of captains. If there is anything gracious, generous, kind, tender, lavish, and super abundant in love, you will always find it in Him. These forty years and more have I served Him, and I have nothing but love for Him. His service is life, peace, and joy. Oh, that you would enter it at once. God help you to enlist under the banner of Christ, even this day."[4]

Those are wonderful words, aren't they? But they are more than fine words. What is so wonderful about quotes from men like Charles Spurgeon, Frederick Faber, and others is not only what they say about Christ, but the fact that their lives proved what they said. Their entire ministries were fashioned by a sight of Christ.

When we explore periods of spiritual health in the church, we don't find just a few isolated statements about Christ. Entire books were written. Books are always a good thermometer of the age in which they are authored, especially books of a religious nature. During seasons when the church is healthy, the books that are the best sellers are the books that speak most of Christ. These books demonstrate that Christ-oriented Christianity is the norm, and self-oriented Christianity is not. If Christ is not the throbbing heart of our focus, we do not possess biblical Christianity.

Let's stop and consider a few examples of these books. Philip Schaff was a highly esteemed professor and theologian. Toward the end of his life, he gathered the best hymns in Christendom and put them in a volume called *Christ In Song*. Every song in this unique collection is about Jesus. Isaac Ambrose wrote the book, *Looking Unto Jesus*. It's a hefty seven hundred pages of tiny print. Each section of the book deals with some aspect of Christ's person and work. After a chapter expounding some aspect of Christology, Ambrose lists the following applications: knowing Jesus in this way, considering Jesus in this way, desiring Jesus in this way, hoping in Jesus in this way, believing in Jesus in this way, loving Jesus in this way, calling upon Jesus in this way, and conforming to Jesus in this way. Can you imagine being so concerned about applying a chapter you read about Jesus that you would go through all eight of those applications to make sure that what you learned in the chapter was not wasted?

Here are a few titles from other Puritan pastors: Robert Asty wrote *Rejoicing in the Lord Jesus in All Cases and Conditions*. Thomas Vincent wrote *The True Christian's Love to the Unseen Christ*. Another, written by Thomas Doolittle, is titled *Love to Christ Necessary to Escape the Curse at His Coming*. (In this book, Doolittle writes that if love to Christ is necessary to escape the curse at His coming, then we must get straight in our minds exactly what God considers love to Christ. Hence, the first half of the book contains fourteen chapters explaining what real love to Christ is). Finally, Philip Henry (the father of the famous seventeenth century Bible commentator, Matthew Henry) wrote a book called *Christ All in All*. The book contains forty-one chapters, each based on some passage of Scripture that describes what Jesus is to His Church—her King, Captain, Priest, Foundation, Food, Light, Banner, Life—to mention a few.

Why did these men spend so much time and energy on the topic of Jesus? They understood that knowing Jesus, loving Jesus, and following Jesus are not simply small parts of the Christian life. They are not even large parts of the Christian life. This *is* the Christian life. To know God in Christ—to be preoccupied with the glory of God as viewed in the face of His Son—that is Christianity; that is life.

What has happened to us?

It would be hard to prove that we live in a day when the most interesting thing a local church has to offer, the thing it promotes most on its website, is Christ Himself. Many of us have spent a lifetime listening to sermons and yet we have never heard one serious sermon series on the glory of Christ. We hear a lot about Jesus, but it tends to be about the things Jesus can do for us. Have we ever really given careful study to those Old Testament passages which most clearly reveal Christ? How many of us have deliberately and carefully studied the gospels to see Christ from all four angles? Have we ever gone to the epistles and ransacked them for their explanations of Christ? When we read the book of Revelation, do we resist the common and less important questions such as, "What's going to happen in the end times?" and "Where is my country going to be?" preferring instead to ask, "God, will you show me the glory of the victorious Lamb?"

What are the titles of the books that are written in our day? A quick walk through a Christian bookshop might reveal top-selling titles like these: "How to Find Contentment," "How to Find True Love," "How to Find Joy," "How to Rescue Your Marriage," "How To be the Man You're Supposed to Be," and "How to Live Your Life to the Fullest Right Now." While these books are not necessarily bad, they reveal that we are a people whose focus is not on Christ. When this sermon was being written, only one of the twenty top sellers was primarily about Christ—and that one focused on following Christ, not Christ Himself. The truth is, all the problems these books are trying to fix are the consequence of people focusing on themselves, on their entitlement, instead of focusing on Christ.

As we rethink God and how we view His Son, it is important to remember that we cannot hold low views of God without also lowering our view of Christ. Nowhere are the results of low and unbiblical views of God more heartbreaking than in this one terrible fact: The churches are, for the most part, uninterested in Christ. The general condition of Western Evangelicals is simple—bored with Jesus, they scratch about to find something in Christianity that they find appealing and hope will appeal to others.

Think of Jesus for a moment. What does the Scripture say Jesus is to His Church? He is all the fullness of God, all the majesty, all the bigness, the eternity, the power, the wisdom, the holiness, the glory of God, coming down and invading human history, united to the human body and soul of Jesus of Nazareth, fully God, fully man. In Jesus, we don't merely see the majesty of God, we see the tenderness of God, the humility of God, the pity of God, and the compassion of God. In fact, we see all the attributes of God reaching out and exerting themselves for the rescue of people like us. Jesus is the sweetest sight of God that the Christian is given.

Have you ever considered the impossibility of having a right view of the Person and work of Christ without the foundation of a biblically recalibrated view of God? If we have a small and inadequate view of God, how can we have an adequately large view of the God-man, who has all the fullness of God? You cannot know the God of the Bible without knowing Christ, and you cannot know Christ correctly until you begin to rethink God.

One problem we have, of course, is that we think we are big enough to know God on our own. We think if we have our Bible and our books and we study them carefully, that we can know God. The truth is that God is too far, too high, too holy, too incomprehensible, too *other* than us for us to know Him by our efforts alone. Yet, He has chosen to make Himself knowable through His Son. The invisible God is now visible. The transcendent God is Immanuel, "God with us." John 1:18 states, "No one has seen God at any time. The only begotten Son, who is in the bosom of the Father, He has declared Him." In 2 Corinthians 4:6, Paul writes, "For it is the God who commanded light to shine out of darkness, who has shone in our hearts to give the light of the knowledge of the glory of God in the face of Jesus Christ." In John 14:9 Christ Himself asks his disciple, "Have I been with you so long, and yet you have not known Me, Philip? He who has seen Me has seen the Father; so how can you say, 'Show us the Father?'" In Hebrews 1:3, we find Christ described as the brightness of God's glory and the express image of His Person. How is Christ the exact image of His Father? He is the perfect representation of God's character. Without exception, everything we see in Christ's character and actions reflects the Father.

The young Scottish preacher, Robert Murray M'Cheyne, pastored during one of the great revivals of the nineteenth century while he was still in his twenties. When writing about God coming in the flesh and knowing God through Jesus Christ, M'Cheyne says, "He is the brightness of His father's glory and the express image of His Person. All the purity, majesty, and love of Jehovah dwell fully in Him. He is the bright and morning star. He is the Son of righteousness. He is the light of the world. He is fairer than the children of men. His riches are infinite. He could say, 'All that the Father has is mine.' He is Lord of all. All the crowns of heaven are cast at His feet. All angels are His servants. All worlds are His dominion. Behold your God. This is God manifest in the flesh."[5]

Is that how we think of Jesus? Heaven's favorite? The apple of the Father's eye? The object of the saints in heaven's unending praise? The study of the angelic hosts? Would the angels find our church services strange? If they came down from the worship of the enthroned Lamb of God, would they be shocked find us focused on something other than Christ Jesus?

Let's be honest: We all need to start with ourselves. Search your own heart. How much time in the past few weeks have you given to the careful study of texts which give the clearest portraits of Christ? Which of those wonderful old books that speak of Jesus' glory have you most recently been pouring over? Of course, we do not expect non-Christians to understand us when we speak of Christ's beauty. After all, they do not know the Jesus of the Bible. They cannot grasp what it is about Christ that grips us. But, to His own, He is all-in-all. Why, as Christians, do we focus on anything else?

If you can bear an honest examination of your own life, then you will be ready to humbly ask some hard questions of your church (which, of course, includes you). Is your church captivated with the realities of Jesus Christ? Is Jesus the topic of so many sermons and conversations that anyone who visited would know that He is what your church finds interesting about Christianity? Unfortunately, when we lose our preoccupation with Christ, we don't quit calling ourselves Christians, close the church doors, and quit attending. We still want to have our church and mention Jesus at the appropriate moments in the service. At the end of the sermon, we still extend a gospel invitation that sounds like "Come down. Jesus died to save you and give you a great life," even if the sermons rarely take the time to explain Him and His work. Is the occasional mention of Jesus really a Christ-centered church service? Is your church treating Christ as if He is merely the doorway into forgiveness and spiritual happiness, and that is all? After baptism, do our converts feel free to make as much or little of Jesus as they desire? This kind of Jesus is not found in the Scripture. He is a reinvented Jesus. He is an idol.

How do we protect our churches from this type of idolatry? First, we need to back up and get the biggest picture of Christ, of the cosmic proportions of the Son of God, that we can. We do not start with the smaller issues of what Jesus can do for us. Second, we need to reject the sentimental Jesus who has been invented by people—the Jesus of Christian movies, Christian romance novels, and t-shirts. We want the true Christ of Scriptures before whom men, women, and angels are compelled to fall down and worship. The Christ of the Bible will not share your heart with the Jesus of your culture. Third, we don't want dim and fuzzy views of Jesus. Vague impressions of Him will never be enough to live upon. Life in a world like this requires crystal clear views of His unique Person and work. This includes more than getting our doctrine correct. We need a living, personal, daily, real knowledge of Christ. Colossians 1 is a wonderful place to start. In this passage, Paul gives us some of the most sublime descriptions of our Lord that we find anywhere in the Bible.

He is the image of the invisible God, the Heir of creation, the Creator of all, the Sustainer of all, preexisting all. He is the Head of the church, the Firstborn from the dead, the beginning of the resurrection. He is the preeminent One with all the fullness of God. What if we were to go back and devote serious time as individuals and churches to unfolding each of these great themes?

In conclusion, consider two questions that serve as warnings. First, will you determine to know Christ, whatever the cost? Take to heart Isaac Ambrose's advice: "[D]on't stop short because of the cost. Whether pains or study, tears or prayers, peace or wealth, goods or reputation, life or liberty, sell them all for this pearl. Christ is so valuable that you can never buy Him, though you gave yourself and all the world for Him. Do not let any cost make you stop short of pressing on to really knowing God through Christ."[6] Second, why not determine to know Christ better than you know any other person? Even better than you know your spouse, your children, or your best friend. Why not begin the lifelong pursuit that will not end at the end of this life? You will want to gather teaching from the clearest passages on Christ and memorize the most helpful hymns and the greatest quotes on Christ. Treasure these words and plead with God, "Show me your Son." Put away the fear of boredom. Will focusing on one Person all the time get boring? No. Spurgeon said, "The more you know about Christ, the less you'll be satisfied with superficial views. The more deeply you study His life and the fullness of His grace, the more truly you will see the King in His beauty."[7] Are you ready for that?

[1] Isaac Ambrose, *Looking Unto Jesus* (United States: Loomis & Co., 1832), 8.
[2] Ambrose, *Looking Unto Jesus*, 302.
[3] Frederick Faber, *All for Jesus Or, The Easy Ways of Divine Love* (United States: John Murphy & Company, 1892), 13.
[4] Lewis Drummond, *Spurgeon: Prince of Preachers* (United States: Kregel Publications, 1992), 288.
[5] Robert M'Cheyne, *The Works of Rev. Robert Murray M'Cheyne* (United States: Robert Carter and Brothers, 1874), 436.
[6] Isaac Ambrose, *The Works of Isaac Ambrose* (United Kingdom: n.p., 1799), 393.
[8] C. H. Spurgeon, *Devotional Classics of C. H. Spurgeon* (United States: Sovereign Grace Publishers, Inc., 2000), 16.

Salvation is not ultimately for our sakes; but for the glory of God. God in salvation is vindicating Himself and manifesting Himself to the whole universe. He is displaying His everlasting and eternal glory.

MARTYN LLOYD-JONES

5

BEHOLDING GOD

The Work of Salvation

The process of rethinking God can be compared to a walk along a corridor lined with windows. Each of the windows is a means God has provided so that we may behold Him. We have considered beholding God in the Scriptures, remembering that the Bible is primarily a God-centered book. We have also considered beholding God in the Person of His Son, who is the exact representation of His nature (Hebrews 1:3). Now, we want to look at beholding God in the work of His Son, specifically the work of redemption—His labor for our salvation.

Remember our connected truths: What you believe about God affects what you believe about yourself. What you believe about yourself affects what you believe about sin, and what you believe about God, yourself, and sin then affects what you believe about salvation. One of the sad evidences of our idolatrously small view of God today is how unimpressed church members are with the account of Christ's saving labors. If asked, few church members would say they are unimpressed with the gospel. But, if their lives could speak for them, they would say, "The gospel is admirable, but

I am bored by it. The gospel is outdated, and I want to hear about new things."

What might this attitude of casual disregard for the gospel look like in your life? Imagine being in a new location and attending a good church on Sunday morning. The members invite you to come back for the Sunday evening service. Your first response might be, "Yes, of course, I would love to come back." But what if those members went on to explain that every Sunday evening service is a gospel service? It is likely your response might look more like, "Well, I was going to come back, but now I am not sure. After all, I am already a Christian. I already have peace with God." This is a wrong response and reveals a wrong view of the gospel. The gospel as the Bible presents it is a great mountain range of truths. The gospel encompasses everything from the beginning to the end of all that God does *for* a sinner and all that God does *in* a sinner to bring that sinner to Himself.

Again, consider how wrong views of the gospel affect reactions to new converts. A twelve-year-old girl, whom you have watched grow up in church, comes to you and says, "I want you to know I asked Jesus into my heart last night. I'm saved." What is your response? Generally, it might be something like, "Well, that's nice to hear. I'm encouraged. I'll pray for you." Of course, you might not be gripped by her report because you doubt its authenticity. But you also might have an indifferent response because you have lost sight of the magnitude of salvation. Let's continue our illustration. Now imagine that same girl had spent years practicing gymnastics, preparing herself, sacrificing everything for gymnastics, and she came up to you and said, "I want you to know I've made it. I'm on the Olympic team." Now your response might be "Wow! Now, that is spectacular. You've done a great job. What amazing news!" Do you see how a lack of appreciation for salvation and genuine conversion may reveal your low view of God? A small God makes salvation a small matter.

Rethinking God requires that we also rethink the gospel and the labors of Christ which make that good news possible. The gospel is not merely the good news from God that has potential to save the soul; it is the mirror of the glory of God. It reflects His character. A right understanding of the gospel in turn becomes a telescope that we turn toward God in order to understand Him better. There are two key truths we must face if we are to rethink the gospel as we seek to rethink God.

The first is this: All that God does reflects who He is. It is possible to learn something about a person by watching his or her actions. But watching a person's actions does not necessarily give you an accurate understanding of that person's character because one's actions can be full of contradictions. There are people whom we think of as kind and nice people, but if caught in a bad moment, they could do something unkind. Conversely, there are people we think of as unkind people, who, in the right circumstances, might do something extremely kind.

When we inspect the actions of God, we never encounter that problem. God cannot be inconsistent. His actions are always in perfect harmony with His character. Take, for example, the illustration of watching God at creation. God steps forward and calls all matter into existence. Not just planet Earth, not just our solar system, not just the Milky Way, but all matter comes into existence in a moment *ex nihilo*—out of nothing. Imagine the glories that you might see of God in that one great act. Then, imagine watching God at the judgment with Christ on the throne, calling the great and the small, the dead rising from the graves, and the living joining them. This great mass of souls before Him, He unveils all that they have ever done and thought and spoke. God separates the believers and the unbelievers. Imagine the great authority in His voice when those who have rejected Him are sentenced to hell forever, and those who have embraced Him are brought into paradise forever. In both creation and judgment, God accurately reveals something of His glory. All that God does reveals who He is.

The second truth we want to consider is that God's work in and for the sinner to bring the sinner to Himself is the greatest display of God's character. This rescue of sinners—of all creation—from sin's impact is the clearest window into the character of God. The gospel is the good news. The gospel is everything that is required for you to have peace with God; it is everything needed for you to be delivered from the tyranny of sin; it is everything necessary for you to know Him, love Him, obey Him, and honor Him. All has been provided in eternity past, in this present moment, and in every future day. The greatest display of God's glory is the work of Christ in the gospel, making you a new creation, in whom "old things have passed away…[and] all things have become new" (2 Corinthians 5:17).

There is bad news. The bad news is this: low views of God negatively impact the hope of the gospel for the people who hold those views. Where do you have room for the cross if you have a small view of God? You might think that God is about three-quarters of an inch taller than you, so the room between you and God is only three-quarters of an inch. Under those circumstances, you would only need a cross that was about three-quarters of an inch high.[1] If we hold small views of God, we will also hold such small views of the cross that we treat it as a light matter.

The good news is that the opposite is also true. As we pursue clearer views of God, we elevate our view of the gospel. The process might be described as follows: As God grows greater in our understanding, we begin to have a more accurate view of ourselves. We begin to shrink, and the chasm between us and God feels infinite. The distance between ourselves and God is no longer a small matter, and we find ourselves faced with a crisis—how are we going to fill the gap? How can a God so pure and distant know us as His own? How is it possible that we can know Him? Then we realize that we must pursue biblically informed and ever-clearer views of the gospel to match the improved understanding we have of God.

One of the symptoms of a low view of God and the gospel is the stripping down of the gospel message. Our modern view of the gospel seems to require only one word—the word *saved*. Have you ever wondered why God uses so many words in the Bible to describe the various aspects of our rescue, yet we use only one? *Saved* is a fine word. It is a biblical word. Yet, it is best understood as a word that summarizes redemption, a word that includes a great many other biblical words.

To get a clearer view of God, you need all the words He has given you in Scripture. You need all His words to span the gap between your soul and your Creator—words such as atonement, propitiation, election, drawing, regeneration, faith, repentance, union with Christ, justification, adoption, sanctification, perseverance, and glorification. These are some of the words God uses to describe the salvation of a soul. Of course, the difference between us and God is not that God really likes theological words and we don't. The difference is in our understanding of God. God knows His own magnitude. Because we have a very inadequate grasp of God's magnitude, we are willing to settle for one word: *saved*. It's a great help to us when we stop measuring the gospel by felt needs and the few words that express them. The gospel must be measured by the Author of the gospel. It is as big as God Himself. So, you and I need all the words He gives us to define what is so good about the good news.

Rethinking the gospel causes us to see that God is altogether lovely. In 1 Corinthians 1:23–24, Paul wrote about the gospel: "We preach Christ crucified, to the Jews a stumbling block and to the Greeks foolishness, but to those who are called, both Jews and Greeks, Christ the power of God and the wisdom of God." Paul describes Christ as the power and the wisdom of God. Paul's description of Christ is in connection with the gospel and the cross. Christ is the Savior. The salvation of a soul is the great demonstration of the power of God and the wisdom of God. Let's consider how we see God's wisdom and power more clearly as we study the gospel.

God is the only all-knowing Being. He "knows [all things] instantly and with a fullness of perfection that includes every possible item of knowledge," past, present, and future, and He knows them without effort.[2] God cannot add to His knowledge. He cannot benefit from instruction. He does not reason through a problem to come to a solution. He never errs in His judgment. The wisdom of God is seen when He takes all this limitless knowledge and applies it perfectly to any situation. He has the skill to take what He knows and bring it to bear upon all matters. This will be seen as we study the gospel.

What about the power of God? The seventeenth century pastor, Stephen Charnock, said, "The power of God is that ability and strength whereby He can bring to pass whatsoever He pleases. . . He is able to do whatever He is able to will."[3] We don't know anyone else like that. Other people can accomplish amazing things, but God can do all His pleasure effortlessly! He can never experience any external limitation of His actions. Psalm 62:11 states, "Power belongs to God." It is part of His essence. The author of Psalm 89 asks, "Who in the heavens can be compared to the LORD? Who among the sons of the mighty can be likened to the LORD?...O LORD God of hosts, who is mighty like You, O LORD?" (Psalm 89:6, 8). The twentieth century theologian, Arthur Pink, in his book, *The Attributes of God,* wrote, "He who cannot do what he will and perform all his pleasure cannot be God."[4] Is that your God—a God who can do all He desires and who constantly performs all His pleasure without limitation?

The true rescue of a sinner is from beginning to end a wonder-filled display of the wisdom and power of God. It began with the Person of our Savior. Think of Him and His birth in the city of Bethlehem. To rescue sinners, the Redeemer had to be God because there is no man, woman, or angel who could have carried the load He was required to carry. But, in order to rescue those from Adam's fallen race, He Himself had to become one of us, yet without sin. He had to be fully and truly human. How could deity and humanity be united? Remember, the angel announced to Mary that Christ would come through her by saying, "The Holy Spirit will come upon you, and the power of the Highest will overshadow you" (Luke 1:35). It is the exercise of an unlimited divine power and wisdom that caused the deity of the Son of God to be united to our humanity in the womb of Mary. Imagine taking all the energy of our sun and bringing it down into one grain of sand. Imagine doing this in a way that the grain of sand could actually contain this energy and not be consumed or destroyed. Our scientists don't have the wisdom or the power to perform such an act. The birth of Christ was a bringing down of all the fullness of the unlimited God—the immeasurable, boundless, incomprehensible, incomparable God—and uniting it to a human soul and body. This act required all power and all wisdom, not just great power and great wisdom. Salvation is from the very beginning a display of the power and wisdom of God because of the Person of Christ.

This display continues with Christ's labors. The first Adam was required to obey God in a perfect environment, possessing a perfect humanity (no sin), with the perfect wife. He still fell. How unlike the labors of Christ! Christ, the last Adam (as the apostle Paul calls Him in 1 Corinthians 15:45), was required to obey all of God's law without one slip. He had to do this in a hostile environment, in a sinful home, surrounded by sinful friends, while attending a sinful "church." Remember, the religious leaders in His denomination were the ones who called for His crucifixion. In the midst of all these hindrances, Christ perfectly obeyed God's perfect law.

There is more! Consider the death and resurrection of Jesus. Never before had a human experienced the unrestricted wrath of God. Jesus of Nazareth passed through the great sea of the God's righteous anger. He drank the cup of the Father's justice to the dregs (no drop was left in the bottom of that cup), and yet was raised victorious, never to die again. It required infinite power to endure the wrath of God. The cross of Jesus is one of the clearest displays of God's wisdom and power.

God's wisdom and power are also on display when He sends Christ to conquer on two battlefronts—our enemies and our own souls. Christ Himself described the battlefront of our enemies in the parable of the strong man (Matthew 12:29). Imagine a strong man who lives in a fortress. Inside the fortress, there is a great treasure which he jealously protects. He is constantly armed and ready. Unless a stronger man comes and conquers the strong man and binds him, the treasure of the house will never be removed. Eventually, a stronger man does come and conquers the strong man, binds him, and loots his house. This picture portrays Christ and Satan. Satan holds the souls of humanity, but Christ conquers Satan on the cross, comes into that fortress, and takes His people from the prison of sin and death. What a great display of power! Even so, that is not enough to rescue us.

Christ also fights on the battlefield of our souls. Jesus must display wisdom and power in conquering each individual sinner. You must be conquered in order to be rescued. Think of what John writes about all of us in John 3:19–21. We do not want Christ's spiritual light. We hide from God in our shame. We prefer the darkness of half-truths and lies instead. We have no appetite for holiness. We are enslaved to self-will and selfishness, and Christ meets us and conquers us. Perhaps you don't think you are that bad off. Sometimes preachers give us a false impression of our condition. They say, "Well, this is the way it is. You're like a person who was in a boating accident. You're far from land and you're hurt. You have a broken arm, broken leg, and you can't swim to the shore—but you can cry out. As your strength fades, you flail around in the water and cry for help. Christ is there on the shore. He hears the cry. He grabs a life preserver and throws it out to you. You, with the last strength that you have, swim over and grab the life preserver and are pulled to safety." Is that what salvation is? The Bible describes a very different scene. If we could use the same illustration, you are like a person who was in a boating accident, but you've been knocked unconscious. You're face down in the water. You don't cry out. You don't struggle. You don't search for someone who will rescue you. You are careless of your danger. Christ, seeing the accident, comes for you, grabs you, and brings you safely to the shore. The illustration isn't perfect, but it demonstrates an unpleasant fact: Your rescue rests upon the power and the wisdom of God—not on your good intentions, nor even on your desire to be rescued. You had to be conquered.

Now, the power and the wisdom of God are seen not only in what Christ brings us out of, but also in what He brings us into. He brings us to live in a new realm—the realm of grace (Romans 5–6). We are free to live for Him. He brings us under a new Master. We are no longer the slaves of sin and death, but of the Son of God, the Son of His love. He dresses us in new clothing. We no longer wear our old rags of self-righteousness. We are no longer just trying to "do better." Now we are clothed with the righteousness of Christ. He gives us a new family and a new name. No longer *in Adam*; now, we are *in Christ*. He gives us a new nature where our heart is soft and receptive to God. We know that one day He will complete the work of glorification in us. Paul wrote from jail to the Philippians, "Jesus Christ…will transform our lowly body that it may be conformed to His glorious body, according to the working by which He is able even to subdue all things to Himself" (Philippians 3:20–21). The power of God that will be exercised in subduing all creation to the rule of Christ is the same power that will be exercised in completing the work of your salvation. The fragments of your sin, your struggles, your disappointments, even your body will be brought into perfect conformity with Christ. Everywhere you look in the work of salvation, you behold the splendor of God.

We have to be honest. It is not easy for religious people to rethink the Gospel. Paul didn't find it easy. Saul of Tarsus once had very inadequate views of what a believer is. He thought you were right with God by your birth into the right ethnic family, by the right education, and by keeping the right rituals and rules. When Saul met Christ, how different things became. He had to reject all he thought before. He had to rethink not only God, but the way of salvation. Three years after Paul first met Christ, he came out preaching boldly. For three years, he thought through the implications of the glory of God. Paul rejects the claims of those who said they were Christians but whose lives did not reflect the wisdom and the power of God. When he wrote to the young pastor, Timothy, he warned him of those who "[have] a form of godliness but [deny] its power…From such people turn away" (2 Timothy 3:5). A person who claims to know Christ but does not give any evidence that the power of God is at work in him or her is simply not a Christian. What God does will always reflect who He is.

What aspect of God's glory can be seen in the average profession of faith in our churches? If that was all you could see of God, would God appear weak, inconsistent, unwise, confused, or unimpressive? Would you see anything of the wisdom and the power of God? If all you see is weakness, then you are seeing man's converts not God's converts. If this is true of your church, are you going to continue to promote false ideas of conversion? Are you going to say, "Well, this is tragic, but I don't know what else to do about it"? Instead, will you search the Scripture? Will you rethink God and rethink the gospel? Will you begin to rethink the salvation of a soul based upon what God says about Himself? Will you keep searching until you are captivated with the magnitude of His gospel?

[1] I am indebted to Mr. Richard Owen Roberts for this illustration.
[2] A. W. Tozer, *The Knowledge of the Holy*, (New York: Harper Collins Publishers, 1961), 56.
[3] Stephen Charnock, *The Complete Works of Stephen Charnock,* (United Kingdom: James Nichol, 1864), 106.
[4] A. W. Pink, *The Attributes of God*, (United States: Baker Books, 1975), 46.

There is nothing under heaven that can constrain a pious soul like a sense of redeeming love.

CHARLES SIMEON

6

BEHOLDING GOD

The Response of Personal Holiness

Knowing God is the great treasure of Christianity. Where do we go to get to know Him? We get to know Him through the Scripture, a book that is primarily a progressive unveiling of the uncreated God. There, we view Him in the Person of His Son. We view Him in the work of His Son, that mountain range of truths that is the activity of God from eternity past to eternity future, encompassing all that is necessary to bring us to peace with God. We behold God most clearly not in creation, not in judgment, but in the salvation of the sinner—in the gospel.

The question we face now is of utmost significance for the health of the church and the effectiveness of her witness: If we press on to know the Lord, how will it impact our desire and ability to live a godly life? In Genesis, God speaks to Abram and explains what kind of life is required of a man who would live near God. Genesis 17:1 says, "When Abram was ninety-nine years old, the LORD appeared to Abram and said to him, 'I am Almighty God; walk before Me and be blameless.'" When the Israelites were brought out of slavery and away from the corruption of Egyptian idolatry, God commanded them, "Consecrate yourselves therefore, and be holy, for I am the LORD your God. And you shall keep My statutes, and perform them: I am the LORD who sanctifies you" (Leviticus 20:7–8). In 1 Peter 1:14–16, Peter tells persecuted Christians in Rome to live "As obedient children, not conforming yourselves to the former lusts, as in your ignorance; but as He who called you is holy, you also be holy in all your conduct, because it is written, '*Be holy, for I am holy.*'" Paul wrote to the new church plant in Thessalonica, "For this is the will of God, your sanctification" (1 Thessalonians 4:3). The writer of Hebrews, giving a mixture of glorious portraits of Christ and terrifying warnings, makes this application, "Pursue peace with all people, and holiness, without which no one will see the Lord" (Hebrews 12:14). *Holiness*. Few words seem so inherently Christian to us, and yet, for all our talk about it, for all our books on it, the world is not impressed with Western Christianity's holiness. Why is this?

At times in the past there were wrong views concerning holiness which produced an unattractive self-righteousness. Rigid schemes for purity were embraced but too often they only produced hypocrisy. We have no interest in going back to that kind of "holiness." Perhaps you have the idea that holiness is something like a bitter antibiotic pill for the Christian. We have the infection of sin, and we must take this unpleasant pill every day to fight the infection. We do not like it, but because we are Christians, we must do it. Western civilization is facing a moral crisis. Two extreme responses to this crisis have surfaced among church attenders. Both responses are flawed because neither are built on a biblically recalibrated view of God.

What are these two responses? The first response comes from the young and restless crowd. They believe that outward separation from the world is no longer necessary. In fact, it is not only unnecessary, but also unhelpful. Those who respond in this way believe that in order to reach the lost world, to penetrate the inner cities, and to bring the twentyish-year-olds into the church, we need to stop emphasizing the distinction between the believer and the unbeliever. We need to appeal to their cultural appetites. Along with this, of course, comes the wrong application of the biblical truth that God has made us free in Christ. This skewed application implies that old appetites do not have to be abandoned. Members of this school of thought can be found walking as close to the edge of sin as possible, under the banner of *grace*.

The second wrong response to our modern moral crisis might be best described as isolationism. This approach is an effort to re-emphasize the importance of holiness. Outward separation from this world is stressed. It is considered the only way to guarantee the purity of our children. The thinking of this response is as follows: If only we can isolate ourselves from the sinful germs of our communities, then we will be holy. So the separation begins. This group will always choose to homeschool, but for many of them homeschooling is not enough. Some start their own home church because modern churches are full of sinners.

We need to be careful—not all who are young and in earnest about reaching the world are against moral separation from the world's ways. Not all who homeschool or worship in a home are isolationists. And people influenced by each of these approaches are often dead serious about religion. Most of us attend a church that is stuck somewhere in between these extremes. We may feel like a ship without a theological anchor, caught between two great storms—the storm that says outward separation is unnecessary and unhelpful, and the storm that says isolation is the only hope.

But these misguided approaches are only symptoms. The root problem is not that we are confused about holiness. If that were the real problem, we could simply buy and read old books on the topic of holiness. We could go to our Strong's Concordance or to the back of our Bible and look up every place where the word holy, holiness, sanctify, or sanctification appears. But we aren't merely confused about holiness, and learning about it won't be enough to solve the real problem. Our real problem is that our view of a holy life is warped because our view of God is inadequate. Our light, modern view of God has produced anemic Christians with no strength to stand against temptation. In his book, *The Knowledge of the Holy*, A. W. Tozer wrote, "It is impossible to keep our moral practices sound and our inward attitudes right while our idea of God is erroneous or inadequate. If we would bring back spiritual power to our lives, we must begin to think of God more nearly as He is." [1]

Rethinking God—not just getting correct doctrine, but really knowing Him—beholding God in all His majesty and His greatness as well as His goodness—is the first step in promoting real holiness. Real holiness is the holiness that is biblically informed, attractive, and comes from union with Christ. God is the beginning of all genuine holiness. What God does is the foundation of holiness. Sin separated all humanity from contact with the one Being who is pure, and we have become accustomed to unholiness. Sin is the atmosphere in which we live. In the book of Job, Job looks across the land and says, "What is man, that he could be pure? And he who is born of a woman, that he could be righteous? If God puts no trust in His saints, and the heavens are not pure in His sight, how much less man, who is abominable and filthy, who drinks iniquity like water" (Job 15:14–16). We will never be able to even step onto the path of holiness by our clever ideas or our willpower. We do not have what it takes to make our own hearts holy, but God does. He makes every single one of His children holy.

The Old Testament foretold that the work of Christ would guarantee that every Christian would have a transformed life—holiness begun. In Jeremiah 31, God says, "This is the covenant I will make with the house of Israel after those days, says the LORD: I will put My law in their minds, and write it on their hearts; and I will be their

God, and they shall be My people" (Jeremiah 31:33). In Zechariah 14:20–21, there is a new breadth of impact foreshadowed. God says through the prophet, "In that day," (referring to the work of Christ in the new covenant), "'HOLINESS TO THE LORD' shall be engraved on the bells of the horses. The pots in the LORD's house shall be like the bowls before the altar. Yes, every pot in Jerusalem and Judah shall be holiness to the LORD of hosts." The wonder of this picture is that even common things, which were excluded from the idea of holiness, would one day be included through the work of Christ: even pots and the bells on farm-horse harnesses.

This is a good time to stop and ask: How holy is your everyday life because of Christ? In modern language, how holy is your car because of Christ? How holy is its stereo? How holy are your pots and pans, your casserole dishes, or your microwave? So, holiness is not just a theme of the old covenant, it is also the goal of God's work for you in the new covenant. The new covenant does not promise a holiness that is less rigorous than that of the old covenant. The new covenant does not lower all of life down to the secular, common level; instead, it raises all the common areas of the Christian life up into the act of worshiping God. Everything can now be a part of living for Him. In 2 Corinthians 5:15, Paul writes, "... He [Christ] died for all, that those who live should live no longer for themselves, but for Him who died for them and rose again." Again, in Ephesians 1:4, Paul writes "Just as He [God] chose us in Him before the foundation of the world, that we should be holy and without blame before Him in love."

The word c*hose* in Ephesians 1:4 is the same word that is also translated *elected.* The process of election is common in our country. If you are a candidate for an office, you have a different freedom than someone who has already been elected and is serving in an office. A person who has been elected has taken an oath of office. He or she has duties to perform. You have been elected. Christian, you are not simply a candidate for holiness, but you have already been elected to be holy.[2] Holiness is the reason for which God chose you in Christ.

We must realize that God Himself defines holiness. He is the standard. We frequently compare ourselves to others, but these comparisons are not spiritually helpful. We can ask what other people do, what other denominations do, what other churches do, what other parents do, or what other students do. But who gets to say who's right? There are two popular options for religious people when we think of the standard and definition of holiness. Those two options are cultural Christianity or the character of God Himself.

If cultural Christianity is our standard of holiness, we will rise to the common level of morality found in the churchgoers around us. You go to Church A, and in Church A, people don't go to movies. They throw their televisions out. So, after a while, in an effort to fit in and be a good Christian, you quit going to the movie theater. Eventually, you throw your television away. You meet their standard of holiness. Now, imagine that your job unexpectedly moves you to another city, and you attend a different church—Church B. In Church B, everyone goes to the movie theater and owns a nice television. For a few months, you might be a little nervous about this church. Eventually, you see that Church B people do love the Lord, and you then adjust yourself to that church. You resume going to see movies. You even buy another television. That is holiness defined by cultural Christianity. You just live up to the standard of the people around you.

When people around us, even churchgoing people, are the standard of holiness, it creates an indifference toward culturally accepted sins. These are sins that are so common in your church that you accept them, even though your God hates them. What are these cultural sins? While examples differ from place to place, there are a few that are very common. These include gossip, greed, vanity, overeating, the need for constant amusement and entertainment, railing against government officials, and complaining about your boss, spouse, or children. You might add sports-centered Sundays where you take your children to their sporting events instead of church because they need to be responsible members of their travelling team. Of course, you lead the group in a five-minute devotion to soothe your conscience. While the community around us may find these sins acceptable, your God hates them. Clearly, because each church has different ideas of which sins are acceptable and which are to be avoided, we cannot use cultural Christianity to define our holiness.

The other option by which to define holiness, then, is God's character. Who God is and the things in which He delights define true holiness. Holiness is simply being separated *from*, so you can be separated *unto*. Holiness is being separated unto a Person. The character of the Person unto whom you are being separated must determine your understanding of holiness. One of the greatest things you can do to promote holiness is to make sure you have the right definition of the word *God.* God is holy. He is essentially separate from all things, from the vilest man to the highest archangel. Does that sound like an exaggeration? Consider the following. All things fall into two categories: that which is God and all that which is not God. There are only the Uncreated and the created, and there will always exist an infinite gap between the two. That is the essential distance that separates everything and everyone from God. However, God is separate from all things morally as well. Anything that is wrong or contaminated, anything that is spiritually unhealthy, is separate from God. Holiness is defined by God's perfection. He does not need to conform to a standard of moral ethics in order to be holy. He does not follow some set of rules to be able to say at the end of the day, "I have been a holy God today!" Holiness is not even primarily based in His actions. It is what He *is*—He *is* eternally holy, unchangeably holy, essentially holy. Since He is immeasurable in all His perfections, He possesses an infinite fullness of holiness. There is no room for Him to grow more holy. It is not possible for Him to become less holy. His holiness is perfectly interwoven with all He is, all His attributes. In fact, every attribute of God is equally holy. He loves what is pure with a perfect love and He hates what is impure with a perfect hatred. His patience is holy. His power is holy. His desires are holy. His anger is holy. All that He is, separate Him both essentially and morally from all else. A. W. Pink sums this up by describing God as "solitary" in His perfections.[3] There simply isn't anyone else in His category. When we rethink God biblically, we will arrive at the realization that He is the definition of holiness.

God's perfections are not only the *definition of holiness*, but they are also the *motive for holiness*. Motive isn't everything, but it is a critical part of your Christianity. Why do you care anything about living a holy life? What is the attraction of holiness for you? This is an important question. You may have a self-centered motivation. You want to be the type of person both you and others can admire. You may not even mind being disliked by people as long as they dislike you because you are so pure and they are so impure. If this is the case, you are using God and His rules to polish your life. That type of polish is really no more than human morality. The difference between morality and holiness might be stated this way: Morality of this type can be defined as what you do or what you refuse to do for your own benefit. Holiness is a separation to the Person of God, motivated by love to God.

The symptoms of me-centered holiness or morality are easy to spot. Holiness becomes your idol when it is a self-centered pursuit. You want to become a better person, and you become bitter with people who do not help you achieve that. You find yourself abandoning the friends who don't help you achieve this goal. You avoid family who are not as holy as you are. Let me give an illustration: Imagine a mother who, when she was young, lived a loose life. At some point, she and her boyfriend decide to get married, and they continue to live the party life. Then they have a child, and they look at the child and think, "You know, we need to be a little more serious now. It's time to grow up. We need to be in church." They go to a church, and she listens intently. She's determined to be a good mom. Listening closely, she hears a long list of bad things from the Bible that she's done wrong and a long list of good things she hasn't done but should. She goes home, buys the best books on how to be a godly mom, how to be a godly wife, how to be a godly young woman. She decides that she's going to change everything. She's going to change the way she's raising her children, the way her family dresses, and even the way they eat. She'd like to get rid of the television, but her husband likes watching it when he comes home from work. She decides to homeschool her children. The couple move out of the city to avoid the crime and start a small farm in the country. She has great plans of holiness for the family, but her husband isn't fulfilling all he needs to fulfill for the dream to come true. She begins to harbor a real bitterness toward this man because he is wrecking the train of holiness that she's trying to keep moving. In the end, she gives up on the whole idea of being a super saint, returns to the old lifestyle, and leaves her husband. She desired a kind of holiness that was all about her. It was her new idol. Anyone that didn't serve her new idol was expendable.

A God-centered motivation for holiness results in a completely different approach. When we begin to rethink God, love becomes the motivation for holiness. When we see God for who He is and we see that He loves us, we are amazed. What Paul said to the Corinthians becomes true of us as well: The love of Christ constrains us (2 Corinthians 5:14). His love for us puts blinders on us, like a horse would wear when plowing, so that we keep our eyes looking straight ahead. The temptations are still there, and we may still feel tempted, but our hearts are captivated by God. He loves us and His love for us constrains us to obedience. We are happy to lay down our rights for a God who loves us.

God's love for us makes us willing to obey, because His love causes us to love Him. Our love for Him, in turn, produces obedience. In John 14:15, Jesus says, "If you love Me, you will keep My commandments" (NASB95).[4] Thomas Chalmers said that there is an expulsive power in the new affection.[5] That is how a nineteenth century Scottish theologian says what today we would say like this: "There is a power to throw out all the old lovers (sins) when God creates a new love for Him in the soul." He takes away the stony heart and replaces it with a new heart. We see God for who He is. We are shocked by His love for us. But the old lovers still hang about in the hidden places—the dark corners of our minds. We have tried to evict them before. We can't seem to do it. Then, this new love comes in the front door of our life and the old lovers go out the back door. There really is an expulsive power in the new love!

Two people who are equally serious about holiness but are acting on two different motivations produce two very different results. Me-centered holiness looks like a person who is trying to get rid of all the spiritual germs and all the germy people so that he or she can be pure. It's like a person who goes to a hospital and says, "I am not sick. I just want to rent one of your hospital rooms." That person moves into the room and busily sprays down the room with the most powerful disinfectants. He or she puts a sign on the front door that says, "Don't come in here if you have any germs on you." While that life may seem very clean, it is not the kind of life that is very happy. It is sterile.

A God-centered holiness looks more like a home than a hospital room. This isn't a perfect illustration, but I believe it can make the point well enough: Imagine a house with a large family room that is clean but also welcoming and cozy. Imagine God lives in this room, and you desire to enter. He calls you to come to Him, but you can't because you are filthy. You have been playing in the dirt of old sins; you have walked down the path of temptation and are covered in its mud. Even though you are a true believer, adopted into God's family, you cannot enter that room and enjoy His company—His nearness—until you deal honestly with the problem of your sin. You cannot bring your favorite sins into that house! Then, you are honest with God about the sin. He forgives again and sends you to the shower to clean off. He puts the clothes of His Son's perfect obedience on you again. Why are you cleaning up? You will do anything it takes to get clean because you want to enter the room and be near your God who has adopted you into His family. You are happy to be clean because God is the motivation. We need to be careful at this point. I am not describing how you become a member of the family of God. I am describing the daily confession, cleansing, and carefulness that will mark the life of the believer who desires to enjoy God's nearness—to live separated unto the One who has already saved you.

We need to say more. God is also the *way of holiness*. Because holiness is so inseparably connected with dos and don'ts, with right and wrong choices, we tend to skip the relational aspect and go straight to the rules. That approach will not work. It is like trying to sweep a room full of dust. The more you sweep, the more the dust flies up in the air. As soon as you turn around and walk out of the room, the dust falls right back down.[6] All you've done is agitate everything and made a mess. When we rethink God biblically, we realize He is the way of holiness. This does not mean we lead a passive life; if God is the source of holiness, we have reason to be very active. Yet, it does change the kind of activities in which we engage. Two biblical metaphors illustrate this concept. In 2 Corinthians 3, Paul says that a Christian spends his or her time looking intently in a mirror. A mirror in biblical times would have been imperfect, made of polished metal. It reflected a dim image and required focus. Paul is referring to the active focus of our thoughts on Jesus. He goes on to say that when this intent gaze is exercised toward Jesus, "We… are being transformed into the same image from glory to glory"

(2 Corinthians 3:18). Our hearts are like old film in a camera. The shutter of the camera is open, and the image of whatever we've pointed it at is embedded on the film. The longer the shutter is open, the greater the exposure and impact on the film. Our hearts are like that. Our souls are formative matter.[7] When we gaze upon the beauty and the glory of God in His Son, and the shutter of our hearts are kept open toward Him, a transformation is occurring. As we gaze upon Jesus with the love of a believer, we become more like Him.

Along with looking unto Christ, true holiness also means leaning on Christ. In the Song of Solomon, Solomon writes, "Who is this coming up from the wilderness, leaning upon her beloved?" (Song 8:5) The scene he refers to is of a tired woman travelling through a wilderness. It is not an option for her to live in the wilderness. She cannot survive there. This woman is weary. How can she make the journey out of this unsafe place? Her husband comes down into the wilderness, puts his arm underneath her, she puts her arm around him, and, by his help, she can come out of the wilderness, leaning on him with each step. It is a beautifully applicable picture. It is not an option for a Christian to live forever in the constant atmosphere of this sinful world-system. Leaning all our desires, all our need, upon the Savior daily, we journey through this sinful world. In both metaphors of holiness, love is the key. It is love's long look at Christ and love's full leaning upon Christ that comprise the way of Holiness.

Still, there is more we need to say: The God of the Bible is also the *hope of holiness*. Have you become deeply discouraged regarding this whole matter? Are you paralyzed by the despair that you could never have a Christian life that rises above the cultural norm? Begin by rethinking God. As we behold God, we find the foundation of all holiness. God met Abram and said, "Walk before Me and be blameless" (Genesis 17:1). How could a man like Abram walk before God and be blameless? The answer is in the passage: "I am Almighty God" (Genesis 17:1). Like Abram, if we are to walk before God and be blameless, to have integrity, it will require a God who possesses all strength to be our help! Nothing less than that will enable us to live a holy life. In Leviticus 20:7–8, when God speaks to the people about holiness, He essentially says this: "Consecrate yourselves. Keep My statues. Perform them." Then, He reminds them of two truths that give them hope that they can actually obey these commands. God tells them: "I am the LORD your God," and "I am the LORD who sanctifies you." Like the Israelites, if we are to consecrate ourselves to God, our only hope of maintaining any real dedication is the same as their hope: God is our Lord and He sanctifies His people. Paul wrote to the church of Thessalonica, "This is the will of God, your sanctification" (1 Thessalonians 4:3). Later, Paul wrote, "Now may the God of peace Himself sanctify you completely; and may your whole spirit, soul, and body be preserved blameless at the coming of our Lord Jesus Christ. He who calls you is faithful, who also will do it" (1 Thessalonians 5:23–24). If that's the longing of your heart—to be completely separated unto Christ—you have the hope of a God who is faithful to see that it is accomplished in you. As we press on to know the Lord, we find that He's everything with regard to holiness. He is the beginning; He is the motive; He is the standard; He is the way; He is the hope.

[1] A. W. Tozer, *The Knowledge of the Holy,* (New York: Harper Collins Publishers, 1961), viii.
[2] I am indebted to Richard Owen Roberts for this illustration.
[3] A. W. Pink, *The Attributes of God,* (United States: Baker Books, 1961), 9.
[4] *The New American Standard Bible*, The Lockman Foundation (lockman.org), 1995.
[5] Thomas Chalmers, *The Expulsive Power of a New Affection,* (United States: Crossway, 2020).
[6] John Bunyan, *The Pilgrim's Progress,* (London: Hurst, Robinson, and Co., 1820), 28.
[7] I am indebted to A. W. Tozer for this illustration.

Worship is simply a humble preoccupation with God.

CLYDE CRANFORD

7

BEHOLDING GOD

Restoring Worship in Our Lives

Rethinking God biblically requires beholding our God as He has always been, as He always will be, and as He truly is right now. Rethinking God biblically—recalibrating our views of God to fit Scripture—affects every area of the Christian life, including how we worship. Worship is the intentional gaze of the soul, whether as an individual or with other believers; it is the giving of ourselves to the God whom we see revealed in Scripture. Worship is the dedication of our entire selves to God, including the thoughts of our minds, the treasures of our hearts, and the intentions of our wills. Since worship consists of drawing near to God to know Him and consecrate ourselves to Him, His character must dictate our approach.

The book of Psalms provides numerous descriptions of true worship. In Psalm 5:7, worship is depicted as drawing near to God, surrounded by a crowd of mercies. In Psalm 27:4, it is described as dwelling in the house of God in order that we might view His beauty. Worship is defined in Psalm 29:2 as giving glory to God while we ourselves are clothed in His holiness. In Psalm 63:1, it is explained as seeking God earnestly and early, thirsting for God as a person who lives in a desert land thirsts for water. Finally, in Psalm 36:8, worship is portrayed as being abundantly satisfied with the very best of food and the rivers of pleasure which flow from God.

The great mystery of worship is that we are able to approach the holy, living God in a way that is life-giving. Worship is calibrated to the pleasure of God, but you cannot truly worship without finding great benefit to your own soul. Nothing is so beneficial to the believer as pulling away from the distracting noises of life and meeting God, as it were, face-to-face through His Son. Regarding this mystery, St. Anselm wrote: "Up now, slight man. Flee for a little while your occupations. Hide yourself for a little time from your disturbing thoughts. Cast aside now your burdensome cares and put away your toilsome business. Yield room for some little time to God and rest for a little while in Him. Enter the inner chamber of your soul. Shut out all thoughts save that of God and such as can aid you in seeking Him. Speak now my whole heart. Speak now to God saying, 'I seek Your face, Your face Lord will I seek.'"[1]

We tend to forget the centrality of God when we gather in an average Sunday morning worship service, where the greatness and the goodness of God ought to hold our thoughts and desires captive. When the focus of a worship service drifts from God Himself, we inevitably search about for fillers to replace Him. We don't tend to stop being religious. Instead, we begin to center our church services around other things. If Sunday morning is the most notable opportunity that believers have to behold God together, then that is also when you will see the most notorious examples of the ill effects of a low view of God. If nothing about God causes you to be interested in the Sunday morning service, you will be offered one of the church's other activities that you will find more interesting. Hardly anything is missing from the American church, is it? You can find a church that is custom made for you—one that has everything you like and nothing you find unpleasant. There are churches that boast cappuccino bars, concerts, bookstores, fitness classes, sports of every kind, even pottery classes. There are cowboy churches, motorcycle churches, and churches that offer blessings for your pet, performed by the pastor. One thing seems missing from these church offerings: The genuine and sacred offering of ourselves in worship to God.

If you recognize this trend away from a preoccupation with God and are hungering for true worship, what do you do? You go back to the Scripture. You go back to the passages that describe God creating all things from nothing. You go back to the passages that describe the God who triumphed over Egypt's empty idols as He freed His people from Egyptian bondage. You study the pictures of God ruling over all things for His own purposes. You return to the cross, where the Father crushed the Son in a terrifying display of justice. You dwell on the resurrection, ascension, and enthronement of your Savior. You think of the terrors of the day of judgment, and you stand in awe of God's holy wrath as He judges the world and the heavenly company sings His praises. Now, after you have spent some time considering God in those ways, you turn from those scenes and look at the average Sunday morning service. You will find yourself wanting to bring Sunday morning in line with these scriptural scenes.

Let's be more specific. As rethinking God changes our view of worship, there are three fundamental effects.

The first effect is that the question "Why do we gather to worship?" is answered. In Hebrews 10:25, we are commanded not to neglect gathering with other believers. Why? Why do Christians gather on the first day to worship? It's an important question because how we answer that question determines how we approach everything in our corporate worship services. Churches may offer different answers: celebration, evangelization, or fellowship. These answers may sound good, but none of them is the primary purpose God gives us in Scripture. They are secondary. True celebration, evangelism, and fellowship are byproducts of focusing on God. If we focus our worship service primarily on celebration, we will not celebrate in a way that is pleasing to the Lord. If Sunday morning is primarily about evangelizing, then any means to get lost people to attend the service seems justified. Have you ever considered that church can become attractive to people with no interest in Jesus, but it becomes offensive to God at the same time? If our focus is on fellowship, we may become more concerned with knowing and pleasing one another than knowing and pleasing God. True unity and Christian community occur when people love God above all else. You can't truly love God and remain unconcerned about others. Celebration, evangelization, and fellowship are things which flow out of a preoccupation with God. In fact, they are only possible when God is the focus. Without a God-centeredness you must artificially create celebration, evangelization, and fellowship. How many American church services are given to the artificial creation of what God alone can produce?

The Bible is clear about the primary reason for gathering on the first day of the week: We gather to worship. What is a simple definition of worship? Worship is viewing the worth of God and responding to Him appropriately. On an average Sunday morning, we should view the worth of God in the Scriptures and respond to Him in the way we pray and sing, how we interact with each other, and how we live when we return home. Rethinking God affects everything about how we worship.

The second fundamental effect that rethinking God biblically has on our worship is the shift of our focus from the horizontal to the vertical. Worship is primarily a vertical act. It is being preoccupied with God to the point of self-forgetfulness. How much of our time in church is focused almost exclusively on meeting our needs, or the needs of people around us? Does it really matter whether we focus on the needs of God's people or whether we focus on God Himself? Is it that big of a deal how you worship, as long as you do it? In worship, failing to focus solely on God is actually a big deal because the roots of this wrong approach go deeper than worship styles. When our view of God is small, we cannot help but think that He exists to help us. This sets in motion a whole series of choices. Because we think God exists solely to help us, each church service and activity is designed to give God a chance to help us more. People's needs become the focus of the sermon, the special music, and the prayer time. People come to hear sermons that explain how following the principles of the Bible can improve a marriage, rescue a teenager, or lead to a successful business. God may be mentioned in all of these sermons, but only as a useful tool.

A vertical focus is also needed in our prayer meetings. While there is a place for the kind of prayers which focus on the needs of humanity around us, it is not where we should begin. Most prayer meetings are solely given to pleading for people's needs (horizontal) instead of seeking God and His experiential nearness and activity (vertical). A typical Wednesday night prayer meeting might consist of fifteen minutes dedicated to mentioning physical needs. After the long list is given, the preacher calls on someone to pray, and the prayer lasts about two minutes. Finally, the preacher gives a shorter, devotional-type of sermon. Everything is focused horizontally, not vertically. It seems that most of us cannot imagine God wanting us to waste an entire service thinking about Him when there are so many needs all around us. You may be thinking, "Isn't this vertical, God-centered approach selfish?" If so, please consider this: Is it a selfish thing to take a whole Sunday service and just enjoy looking at God? No, it is not selfish. It would be selfish if we came to God and said this, "We are here because we need something from You. We know that You have described what worship is, but we think we have a better idea of how to meet our needs." Which is truly selfish? Focusing on the King who rightfully demands our full attention? Or focusing on the felt needs of ourselves and those around us? Those for whom we pray, interceding for their needs, will not suffer loss because we begin our praying with God instead of them.[2]

Another objection to this type of vertical service is that it does a disservice to the lost. Doesn't it demonstrate a lack of compassion for unbelievers who attend the church service when we focus on God instead of evangelism? The answer is no. We are facing a significant problem in the West, where evangelicalism has dominated the religious culture. People who don't know the Lord have already been introduced to our evangelistic tactics. They know the answers to our tricky spiritual questions. They are not impressed with our invitation at the end of the service in which we promise them everything God has to offer if they simply come forward and repeat a particular prayer. They are not drawn to feel the need for God. They look around and say, "I'm just like you. I'm here on a Sunday morning. I'm glad the preacher is talking about a certain issue today because it is an issue that I'm interested in, and after it's done, I'm going to go home just like you are."

Perhaps we have not sufficiently considered the trueevangelistic impact of a worship service that is focused on God. Imagine that a person comes to church and looks around. He or she sees a group of people who look similar to himself or herself. Perhaps they recognize a successful businessman, or a teacher from their child's school. But these people are preoccupied with God. The sermon is all about God—the preacher focuses on God for the sake of God instead of God's usefulness to man. They see a people who are caught up with God, completely self-forgetful. It is at this point that such a person feels very different than the church people. They don't get it. They don't see what it is about Jesus Christ that makes these otherwise well-balanced people so happy to spend their morning thinking only about Him. After attending a service like that, what defense can a person offer when they find themselves bored by God? What is the explanation for being so different? How does one justify oneself? The person will have to go home saying things like "Why don't I love God like that? I call myself a Christian, but I am not that kind of Christian. Why am I not more interested in God? Why am I not happy to sit through a sermon about God? They can't see Him. They can't hear Him. They can't touch Him. Why are they so captivated by Him?" When we change our worship from horizontal to vertical, God will draw the people to Himself.

A third fundamental effect on worship of rethinking God biblically is a new responsiveness in Christian life that replaces a self-directed initiative. If God is King, then He has the right to dictate how we come to Him. This means we have a choice when we come to church. We are either going to choose to obey the God who has told us how to draw near to Him, or we are going to disobey Him. Strangely, in this matter, both those who obey Him and those who disobey Him still go to church, and both may be in earnest. When God is big and we are small, we feel that a response of precise obedience is an indispensable element in worship. But if we are big and God is small, we will value innovation above responsive obedience. When you read the Scriptures carefully, you will never find God praising those who are innovators in worship.

In fact, idolatry often begins with innovation in worship. An example of innovation leading to idolatry can be found in the book of Leviticus. God rescues the children of Israel out of Egypt to be brought near to Him. These Israelites had the living God in their midst. Hundreds of thousands of Jews camped, all facing the center where the tabernacle was located. In the tabernacle was the Holy Place, and in the Holy Place was the glory of God. No nation had ever enjoyed such privileges. The second half of the book of Exodus and the first eight chapters of the book of Leviticus are dedicated to very specific instructions about what Moses and the people were to do in order that God would dwell in their midst. Every detail was specified, from what kind of hooks were used to hang the tapestries upon the rails, to how the incense was to be burned in the censer as a part of the worship service. Leviticus 8 describes the preparation for worship. Aaron and his sons must go through ritual cleansings and put on the priestly garments. In Leviticus 9–10, on the day when God draws near, they go forward to present the sacrifices. Aaron's sons bring the incense burning in the censers as a sweet smell to God. All the people are watching. God has already manifested His presence in a visible manner. It is a time of great rejoicing because the people have their God with them! As Aaron's adult sons come up to the altar, fire from heaven comes down and kills them both. The crowds gasp and fall on their faces. Moses turns to Aaron, the father who has just seen his sons die, and says, "This is what the LORD spoke, saying, 'By those who come near Me I must be regarded as holy; and before all the people I must be glorified'" (Leviticus 10:3). In other words, God must be treated as holy by those who would draw near to Him.

Why did God destroy Aaron's sons with fire? What was their sin? They had become innovative in worship. In Exodus 30, where the incense is specifically described, God tells the people that they were not to use this particular formula of incense for any other thing. It was just for the worship of God. However, Aaron's sons changed something about the incense. When they brought this innovative form of incense before the altar, God killed them for it. It is dangerous to be an innovator in worship when the King has already told us how to approach Him.

Despite this account, innovation still tempts many church leaders because a great number of people who come to church are bored with God. Horse riding at the cowboy church is much more exciting than long sermons about a God you don't know. Expressive dance teams are preferable to prayer meetings when you don't know God. A traditionalist approach to church isn't necessary biblical, either. In the 1950s, there was a great flood of attendance in the churches and great growth, but these were also days of innovation. Whether the innovation in your church is very traditional—using an approach resembling that of the 1950s—or very modern, the root error is the same. Instead of going back to who God is and allowing that to form our approach to worship, we are going to our culture and asking people what they want.

One of the surest signs that we are rethinking God biblically is that we begin to ask better questions about church. "How can we get people interested?" is replaced with "How are we going to offer to God that which is most pleasing to Him?" Since worship is something we offer to God, God's likes and dislikes must guide our choices. Everything in church, from baby showers to baptisms, should be guided by this thought: What would the God of the Bible want this function to look like? What would please Him most in this church activity?

Another area of worship that is impacted by rethinking God is how and what we sing in worship. A right view of God will produce a carefulness about what we are singing to Him and about Him. We want to sing the songs that give the highest and clearest views of God. We will always fall short, but our goal is to increase the understanding and lift the hearts of the people to worship God as He really is. Many of the modern choruses, as well as many of the old hymns, fail in this area. The songs may sound nice, and they may even stir our hearts, but the words to these songs are careless in their descriptions of God. We must make sure we do not teach people to sing idolatrously low things about God just because of a catchy tune.

When we rethink God biblically, we are also forced to rethink the whole issue of emotion in worship. When God is small and you are big, your emotional response to worship is all-important. In the Scriptures, God warns us that emotions stirred do not equal worship accepted. Just because we feel like we have attended a wonderful service doesn't mean God agrees. Worship is only acceptable when it is done according to God's express desires. We can experience the same types of emotions in other situations. We can go to a good concert and hear music that stirs our hearts. We can go to a movie and experience emotional responses similar to those we feel in church. Now, emotions have a legitimate place in worship. No one can read the Bible and doubt that. Joy should be experienced as we draw near to God, because He is ours and we are His. However, the Bible teaches that the Christian life is not all joy and celebration. There will be solemnity, godly fear, weightiness, grief, and peace. Just read the Psalms and note the wide range of emotions experienced as the believer draws near to worship God. But you will find it helpful to ask yourself, "What is the reason that my emotions are so stirred today?" Are your emotions moved by the realities of God? Does His truth fuel these feelings and guide their expression? It is not easy to be honest about our emotions.

Finally, rethinking God helps us to expand our understanding of the scope of worship. We no longer think of worship as something that happens for an hour on Sunday morning. All of the believer's life is now brought under the reality of God. Every aspect of life—the exciting things and the mundane things—are all now to be offered to God as an act of worship. God is everywhere. God is present at all times. We live before His face whether we are cleaning dishes, driving to work, or meeting together in a Bible study. God is our God and we want to offer Him our minds, hearts, and wills. No hour of the day needs ever be purposeless for the Christian because it can be brought into that wonderful quality of a life of worship.

Start with yourself. In your quiet times, as you open the Bible, you are no longer merely searching for a thought or comforting concept for the day. You are not opening the Bible this morning so that God will tell you which college to go to or which girl to marry or which car to buy. You are opening the Bible primarily to know God, but not merely to know Him. You come to the Bible to see His worth and to respond to it, so your Bible study becomes a time of worship. Then, you bring the realities that you saw in your quiet time into your daily activities. You continue to worship by bringing thoughts of His worth into your memory throughout the day. In this way, your life is spent responding to the living God instead of responding to everything that's happening around you, good or bad. Focusing on God in your quiet time becomes the first act of a day of worship.

Wouldn't it be wonderful if we determined to so rethink God that it would change everything we think about worship? What if we determined to do all that is within our ability to humbly point those with whom we have contact toward the same thing? What if people in churches lovingly said, "I am grateful for what we have here at this church, but I want us to want more of God"? This applies to more than the gathering of believers on Sunday and your personal time alone with God each day. What if family worship time was transformed as well? What if it became a time set apart to know God's worth and to respond to it? In individual, family, or corporate worship, what a magnificent transformation might occur if we rethink God and apply it to our approach. God help us.

[1] St. Anselm, *Proslogium* (United States: Open Court Publishing Co., 1903), 3.
[2] For Jesus' instruction on prayer, and the order by which we come to its different elements, see Matthew 6:9–13.

The great need of every Christian worker is to know God.

HUDSON TAYLOR

8

BEHOLDING GOD

Evangelism

Two thousand years ago, Jesus Christ said to a group of very religious people, "Woe to you, scribes and Pharisees, hypocrites! For you travel land and sea to win one proselyte, and when he is won, you make him twice as much a son of hell as yourselves" (Matthew 23:15). This is quite a shocking statement! Jesus Christ, the seeker of lost souls, turned to the pastors of that day and told them that their evangelism did not make people children of God, but instead made them children of hell. Eighteen hundred years later, America was in the middle of what has been called the Second Great Awakening. While there was much in this movement that was a genuine work of the Lord, the careful men of the day noticed that it was a divided movement. Two theological camps developed. One that moved more toward new techniques—what we might call the beginning of a much more man-centered type of evangelism—and one that held to the evangelistic methods and message of the First Great Awakening. James Alexander, a pastor you may not have heard of, was a faithful and successful minister. He pastored in New York City. It was the site of countless thousands of professions of faith, but professions that had been gotten through a sinner's prayer, which was being used for the first time in America. As he ministered throughout the area, he described the spiritual scene. It was a place where many had professed Christ through the new evangelistic tactics, but ministering there was not a joyful experience. Instead, he described it as a 'burned over district.' It was as if a wildfire had swept across the land and no spiritual life remained. When he spoke to people about Christ, they would tell him that they had already tried Jesus and they were no better for it. They were not interested in trying again. They had become spiritually charred earth.[1]

In the year 2021, a Gallup Poll in the United States of America asked questions regarding religion. About seven out of ten Americans claimed the Christian faith was their religious preference.[2] Can you believe that seven out of ten people you meet in America are living upon the truths of Christ and under His rule? Could you believe seven of ten have been spiritually raised to new life, born to a living hope, and demonstrate it by walking as Jesus walked?

When preachers level their artillery at the problem of evangelism, they usually aim at the problem of non-evangelism. They address the problem of church members being apathetic and failing to talk to people about Christ. While that certainly is a problem, there are other problems. One of the great problems is misguided evangelism—a counterfeit type of evangelism that looks like the real thing, but it is not. Although it is often practiced and promoted by true Christians, it is not true evangelism. We are presently living with the consequences of an evangelistic approach that has been characterized by boldness and cleverness, but it has not always been distinctly guided by the Word and character of God. We have created a mess! We have churches that have been weakened by the influx of great numbers of religious talkers whose lives are unaltered. The world looks at us and mocks us. (Sadly, not all the mocking is unfounded). When the people of the world compare themselves with those who claim to be "born again children of God," they don't see significant differences. The church, instead of dealing with the root problem of its evangelistic approach, runs about tying new fruit to dead trees, hoping that the world will be impressed with the appearance of spiritual success.

It is important to avoid being either unnecessarily critical or critical for the wrong reason. We can have inferior motives for criticizing. We can look around and say, "Our methods aren't working. We're having hundreds of baptisms, but only a few people are actually in the church a year later. We need something new." Instead of criticizing modern evangelistic methods because they are ineffective, our criticism may need to point out that many modern evangelistic tactics are flawed because they do not honor Christ. One modern theologian said, "Don't bemoan the condition of [modern] evangelicalism because it is hollow and therefore weakening.... Instead, bemoan the [modern] condition of evangelicalism because it contradicts the truth of God and belittles His worth."[3] Now, those are two very different reasons to be concerned, aren't they? We do want to see people truly and enduringly saved. However, the greatest problem with misguided evangelism is not that people aren't getting into heaven, it's that it belittles God. You are on the right path of rethinking God biblically when you love the honor of God enough to evangelize and are willing to change how you evangelize if your previous methods misrepresented Him.

As we look at the God of the Bible, we must allow our understanding of Him to change our behavior. Look first on the scenes of worship in the book of Revelation. In Revelation 5:9, the Son is worshipped as the Redeemer. In chapters 11 and 15, we find waves of worship offered to the redeeming, ruling, and judging Christ. After beholding those scenes of glory—those pictures of the Son's eternal rights, claims, and majesty—we can then turn our faces to the lost person and tell them the gospel of that King. We behold

God and allow that to affect everything we do when we witness.

Rethinking God biblically can produce a number of beneficial effects on our understanding and execution of evangelism. We will consider six of these effects.

The first effect can be seen in how we carefully redefine evangelism. A right view of God immediately reveals several things that evangelism is not. It is not just convincing people of the basic facts of the Bible. It is not just bringing people to a decision. It is not convincing them to let Jesus hand them the gift of forgiveness. It is not inviting people to evangelistic church services, special events, or concerts. It is not stealing someone from another church. It is not convincing someone to think like us so that he or she will embrace our denomination's favorite doctrines. That's not biblical evangelism.

What is biblical evangelism? Evangelism consists of explaining the great deeds of God on behalf of the sinner. It is bringing people to a Person, to *the* Person who is the outshining of God's glory—His Son. What good does it do to get on a mountain and say to the people, "Believe and come," if you haven't explained to them what they're supposed to believe and to whom they're supposed to come? Evangelism is telling good news. Stop and consider all that is included in the big picture of this good news. It is telling the deeds of the Captain of our salvation, the Author and Finisher of our faith (Hebrews 12:2). It is sharing the glorious truth that God has appeared in our nature (the mystery of the incarnation), fulfilled the requirements His own law, been crushed under the outpouring of divine wrath as demanded by the broken law, and raised to show all the world that the Father has accepted the Son's sacrifice on behalf of those who were born His enemies. It is explaining the hope of an occupied throne in heaven and the work of the Spirit in bringing the sinner from death to life, resulting in an indissoluble union with Christ by faith. It is sharing a pardon, peace, and purifying, transforming work of the Spirit that cannot be destroyed. It is publicly recognizing Christ the Lord, alone ruling over all the worlds, as your Lord. We, as evangelists, have the task of presenting these grand realities of redemption in a way that we pray God will make irresistible. Rethinking God helps us rethink the *what* of evangelism.

A second effect of rethinking God is that it helps us understand the *why* of evangelism. It affects our motivation. Why are we telling people about Christ? There are two main motives: love to God and love to the lost. There is love to God—the One who has commissioned us to speak to those who live as His enemies, blind and often belligerent. There is also love to the lost soul—the God-hating, self-destroying, rebellious, traitorous soul. Love to God and love to the lost are the two motives that God ascribes to Himself. God loves His honor, and He does all things for His name. God also, amazingly, loves to honor Himself by saving those who hate Him. Keeping those two motives in the correct order is imperative. Love to God will be the soil in which love to others will grow. It cannot be reversed. If we attempt to reverse these then our love to our fellow man becomes warped. We begin to move our allegiance from the holy God to the rebel and begin to treat evangelism like an attempt to get the poor person off the hook with an angry God.[4] That is not evangelism.

Because compassion for the unbeliever has been so frequently the topic of evangelistic seminars, we will turn our thoughts to the other motive: love for God's name—His reputation. The ultimate end of all of God's actions is that His name might be rightly exalted. The idea of God doing all things for His own name's sake sounds strange to us because if we did that, it would be inappropriate and idolatrously self-centered. This is another place where our view of God really starts to show. Do we recognize that God is significant enough to do things for His own name's sake, or do we think He must do everything for us? Do the following verses reflect your view of God?

"I write to you, little children, because your sins are forgiven you *for His name's sake*" (1 John 2:12, emphasis added).

"*For Your name's sake*, O LORD, pardon my iniquity, for it is great" (Psalm 25:11, emphasis added).

"Help us, O God of our salvation, *for the glory of Your name*; and deliver us, and provide atonement for our sins, *for Your name's sake*" (Psalm 79:9, emphasis added).

Paul even writes to the Thessalonians and says that God sanctifies the believer *for His name's sake*. Paul prays that the Thessalonians would obey Christ, "*that the name of our Lord Jesus Christ may be glorified in you*" (2 Thessalonians 1:12, emphasis added).

It's always good to back up and get perspective. Back up from yourself, your family, your lost friends, and the lost church members you see each week. Back up and ask yourself, "What is God doing in the bigger picture?" How many years have you been alive? What has God been doing every year of your life? What has God been doing during the five hundred years since the Protestant Reformation? For two thousand years since Christ's death on the cross, what has He been accomplishing? What's He been doing through every generation of humanity since Adam and Eve turned their backs on Him? Why did He create all things in the first place? While there are many worthy secondary goals in God's actions, the ultimate purpose for which He has been doing everything is to reveal His supreme worth, His superlative glory. "*For My name's sake*" could be plastered above every one of God's actions. Could "*For God's name's sake*" be written over your evangelism?

The third effect that rethinking God will have on our evangelism is that it helps us keep the right audience in front of our eyes. In evangelism, we should always be aware of two people: the lost person to whom we are witnessing and God. Paul explained his approach to the gospel ministry with these words: "We speak in the sight of God in Christ" (2 Corinthians 2:17). Paul never simply spoke to the people in front of him; he was also speaking before an observing God. Consider how a lack of awareness of God in our evangelism has opened the door to questionable tactics. Take the metaphor of fishing. Christ said He will make us "fishers of men" (Matthew 4:19). What does that illustration mean to you? In Jesus' day, the method of fishing was to cast out a net and then pull it in. This is an appropriate picture of evangelism. We bring the gospel to all, casting the net of truth and calling upon people to repent and believe (drawing in the net). God uses these efforts of ours to gather people to Himself. However, for most of us that is not our idea of fishing. Our wrong approaches to evangelism more closely parallel fishing for sport. Modern fishermen use a rod and reel with a line that is nearly invisible to the fish. At the end of this invisible line are clever lures. These flash and move in a way that attract the fish, while hiding the hook. Modern evangelism often attempts to hide the hook—the call to repent, to die to one's delusion of autonomy, to daily deny one's self in preference for others. If we aren't careful, we may drift so far as to justify emotional manipulation, flattery, and every other form of craftiness in order to get people to take the bait. We justify any technique as long as it promises to get more people into heaven. This application of Jesus' metaphor of fishing is not biblical evangelism, and it doesn't get more people into heaven. But regardless of the effectiveness of crafty tactics, as ambassadors from the King of kings, we are only authorized to use means that reflect the King's character.

It is immensely important that we realize that the methods we use in evangelism become part of the message. The method you use will say things about Christ and His gospel long after the people have forgotten your specific words. Do your methods clearly represent your God? The method cannot be chosen by its apparent effectiveness. If there is a clown riding a unicycle on stage on Sunday morning, more children might sit up and pay attention, but does the clown reflect the character of God? Do the kids go away with a clear understanding of their desperate condition and the hope that can be found only in the work of Christ? Or do they go away thinking, "This church is fun"? Consider how your view of God will be reflected and promoted in the type of gospel literature you use. You may have seen the gospel tracts that appear to be fifty-dollar bills. I have seen Christians leave this fake money, along with a couple of dollars, as a tip for the waiter in a restaurant. The waiter comes along at the end of the meal, excited about the tip, and thinks, "Oh, fifty dollars!" He picks it up and unfolds it and reads, "Are you disappointed? Jesus will never disappoint you. Turn this over and read how you can be saved." This may seem clever. Yet have you considered how unlike Christ this tactic is? Did Jesus trick people like that? Was He clever and crafty? Imagine what message that method sends to the waiter. But consider what a wonderfully different message would be communicated if you were to take a moment and tell him in a transparent, vulnerable way, "I want to you to know the Lord who rescued me. Here is a booklet that you might find helpful should you want to learn about Him." As ambassadors, we must be able to be trusted with God's honor in *how* we evangelize, and not merely in *what* we say.

The fourth effect that rethinking God will have on our evangelism is that it will alter where we start with people. It is easy to have the wrong starting place in evangelism. The right place to start is with honesty about our problem. One problem with humanity is that we are already spiritually crammed full! We are full of ourselves, our plans, our rights, our importance. God will not fit into the life of a person who already has everything they want. God can't be added to the life of a self-satisfied person. Consider what Isaiah says about God's dwelling places and how that impacts your understanding of evangelism. In Isaiah 57:15, we read that God has two places where

He dwells, "For thus says the High and Lofty One who inhabits eternity, whose name is Holy: 'I dwell in the high and holy place, with him who has a contrite and humble spirit...'" God manifests His presence in heaven, and in the life of the spiritually contrite person on earth. Much of our evangelism could be described as wasting time trying to convince God to add a third residence: The heart of the spiritually proud. A proud man feels that he has a right to act the way that he's acting. A proud man is full of great plans he has made for his life. Until the proud man is emptied and becomes a humble man, God will never live in him. Christ used the metaphor of a sick person and a doctor to describe this problem. In Mark 2:17, Christ said, "Those who are well have no need of a physician, but those who are sick." That is simple enough. Only sick people want to go to the doctor. Then, he went on to apply it spiritually: "I did not come to call the righteous but sinners to repentance." Have you ever attempted to get people to visit the Great Physician, Jesus Christ, when they think that they are healthy?

Evangelism often starts with the process of emptying. How can a person be emptied? Emptying a person may sound strange, but it is biblical. In Matthew 5:3–6, Christ says, "Blessed are the poor in spirit...Blessed are those who mourn...Blessed are the meek... Blessed are those who hunger and thirst for righteousness, for they shall be filled." There is a progression in this passage. First, God begins to work in a person. As people see God for who He really is, they see themselves as they really are. They become aware of their spiritual poverty. They realize they are poor—bankrupt, in fact—in spirit, and they confess their poverty to God. After this confession is made, they go on to be brokenhearted over what they've seen of themselves. They become meek and humble toward others. After all, how can they remain arrogant toward others when they have faced the truth about themselves? When God strips away what they thought gave them spiritual value, they become desperate for God to intervene. They plead with God not to abandon them to this emptiness. God fills that hungry, thirsty person with righteousness—a righteousness that comes through faith from His Son's obedience.

How can you empty a proud person? Have you ever tried? The best tool Scripture gives for emptying proud, full hearts is God's law. Of course, as Paul reminds us in Romans 7, the law alone never saves anyone. It is not a ladder that can be used to climb to heaven. The law is, however, an effective tool in guiding people to Christ. It is a plow for hardened hearts that prepares them for the seed of the gospel. Paul says the law exposes us for what we really are, aggravates the sin already in our hearts, and condemns our behavior (Romans 7:7–13). God uses the law to lead people to Christ (Galatians 3:24). In early America, during the First Great Awakening, Gilbert Tennent went from town to town, preaching on the themes of God's majesty, the law, holiness, sin, and judgment. George Whitefield, who often worked alongside Tennent, wrote: "It is for preaching in this manner that I like the Tennents. They wound deep before they heal."[5] Tennent understood that until people felt that they did not deserve the love of God, they would never pay attention to the gospel. The law prepares the way for the gospel. It is a waste of time to offer unmerited love to people who think who they are quite lovable. Rethinking God can prevent us from wasting our efforts in evangelism by helping us start in the right place: Emptying the self-satisfied.

The fifth effect that rethinking God will have upon our evangelism is trust. We must trust God in our evangelism. It sounds right; it is right. But it is not effortless. Souls are at stake, maybe even souls that are in our own families. But biblically clear views of God will enable us to trust Him, even with our loved ones. Jesus is our example. He is the one who shows us how evangelism ought to proceed. He brought different truths to bear upon different people, depending on where they were spiritually. He dealt with the woman at the well very differently than He dealt with Nicodemus. The gospel must be carefully applied. We must trust Christ's pattern enough to follow it ourselves. No one who strives to have a high and holy view of God will feel free to disregard the pattern of God's Son. We must learn to trust the Spirit. He convicts. While we tell people the facts of the gospel, it is the Holy Spirit who opens their eyes and gives them faith and repentance. He puts a soft heart within them. He writes the law on the inside. He gives them the new birth, and He alone assures them they are His.[6] Do we trust the pattern of Christ and the power of the Holy Spirit enough to back off and quit playing God? Getting biblically informed views of God will enable us to trust Him.

The sixth and last effect that rethinking God will have on our evangelism is that it gives the right measure of those who witness for Christ. The world mocks a person who honestly talks to other people about the deeds of Christ. After being repeatedly rejected, scoffed at, and pitied by family and friends, we might begin to measure the privilege of being a witness for Christ the way the world measures it, but we must not. Samuel Rutherford, a pastor in Scotland in the seventeenth century, said that gold coins can fall from a pocket onto a dirty path and people can trample them in to the mud but they are still gold.[7] Those who witness for Christ may be trodden into the dirt in our day, but they still have great value to God. In 2 Corinthians 3, Paul said that the superiority of the new covenant meant that the privilege of sharing Christ was far superior to Moses' old covenant privilege of ministering the law. Paul went on to use the contrast between the fading glow on Moses' face (after God spoke to him) and the unfading glory of the new covenant. It is the same for every believer. Every Christian is able to turn to someone and tell them about the finished work of Christ, which is a greater privilege than Moses had in telling the Israelites about the law. Paul wrote, "Since we have this ministry [in the new covenant], as we have received mercy, we do not lose heart...But we have this treasure in earthen vessels, that the excellence of the power may be of God and not of us" (2 Corinthians 4:1,7). The only way to see what Paul saw about the privilege of evangelism is to see it in light of God's greatness as viewed in His Son in the new covenant.

We have been given a great trust as Christians. We have been given the gospel. As we are reintroduced to the God of the Bible, we turn from the splendor of who He is to the lost soul sitting next to us. Our evangelism is recalibrated by that view of God! For the glory of God and for the love of that soul, we tell them the great deeds of Jesus Christ. More than we need another class on evangelism, or a new gospel tract that answers all the unbeliever's objections, we need to know our God.

[1] Iain Murray, "Chapter 13," in *Revival and Revivalism: The Making and Marring of American Evangelicalism, 1750–1858* (United Kingdom: Banner of Truth Trust, 1994).
[2] Jeffrey Jones, "How Religious Are Americans?," Gallup.com (April 19, 2022), https://news.gallup.com/poll/358364/religious-americans.aspx.
[3] John Piper*, A Mind in Love with God* (Annapolis, Maryland: The Jonathan Edwards Institute Conference, July 3, 1997).
[4] For a penetrating criticism of man-centered sympathies in evangelism and missions, consider the sermon, "Ten Shekels and a Shirt," by Paris Reidhead.
[5] Arnold Dallimore, *George Whitefield: The Life and Times of the Great Evangelist of the 18th Century Revival* (Oxford: The Banner of Truth Trust, 1989), 490.
[6] Ezekiel 11:19; John 16:8; John 3:1–36
[7] Samuel Rutherford, *Letters of Samuel Rutherford*, ed. Andrew Bonar (United Kingdom: Oliphant, Anderson & Ferrier, 1891), 127.

I must work the works of Him who sent Me.

JOHN 9:4

9

BEHOLDING GOD

Our Christian Service

God has entrusted the Christian with the greatest treasure: The truth about Himself. The world doesn't understand God and is often unwilling to listen to the church when it speaks about His character. But God has not only entrusted the Church with the truth about Himself; He has also provided many beautiful ways of taking this truth to the world. One of the means He has provided for the world to see Him is our Christian service. Because it is His truth and His means for recommending that truth, we must be very careful that our service clearly reflects who God *actually is*. That is, our service is to be distinctly Christ-like, not merely humanitarian. In fact, our Christian service should be as far from mere humanitarianism as it is from a lazy, self-centered life. To serve God and others in this way, we need to go back to the Scriptures and see God as He really is: Enthroned above all and the Object of highest adoration. After a long look at God, we will be ready to look at the needs of those around us. This will allow His character to fashion everything about our service—what we do and how we do it. Neither the felt needs of those around us nor our own personal preferences, for or against certain types of service, can be our guide. Our goal must be to meet human needs in a way that is in keeping with the character and the purposes of God Himself.

A spiritual Copernican[1] Revolution is needed when it comes to our Christian service. Strangely, a man-centered approach must be replaced by a God-centered one. What is Christian service? It can include all the commonplace tasks that express kindness, compassion, and helpfulness: hospitality, writing a letter, making a phone call, hospital visits, caring for an elderly parent, helping an overwhelmed young mom, keeping nursery in church, teaching a Bible study, befriending a young person at church whose parents aren't believers, going on a mission trip, constructing churches, tutoring children after school, or feeding the hungry, to name a few. If you are willing to work, the list appears endless. In Christ, we see the incarnation of all the beauty, goodness, and righteousness of God's character, living among us as the great Servant of the Lord. Every act of kindness Jesus performed reflected the character of His Father. That is the pattern for every Christian.

In this matter of service, Christ has called you to be a follower—an imitator—not an admirer. You are not merely a pupil who sits in a room at a desk with a Bible, computer, and coffee, writing down what Christ says. Instead, you are an apprentice. You come to the Master to be taught. He brings you alongside Him in His ongoing work through the church. We could say He puts His hands over your hands and teaches you how to do the things He calls you to do in the way He did them. You will learn on the job. Another way of stating this is to say that God sends you in the same way that Jesus was sent. In John 20:21, Christ says to the eleven apostles, "Peace to you! As the Father has sent Me, I also send you." This principle applies to every believer. You are not among those eleven apostles, but wherever He sends you, whatever mundane tasks face you today, you should do them according to the pattern you see in the

God-man. It may sound mystical and mysterious. It is not. John's Gospel, in particular, gives us clear indications of how to follow Christ in this. In it, we see that Jesus depended on God and yielded to God—a pattern that is imitable for every believer. No aspect of the pattern of Christ's earthly life which you are called to imitate requires that you be God. Jesus, both King and Servant, has delineated the pattern for service in His kingdom. He has defined it by teaching and reinforced it by example. Rejecting that pattern and choosing a different one—no matter how sincere and well-meaning—is an act of rebellion against God. Acting outside of that pattern means your service is no longer truly Christian. It is merely humanitarian. In the *Memoir and Remains of the Rev. Robert Murray M'Cheyne*, M'Cheyne wrote, "It is not great talents God blesses so much as great likeness to Christ."[2]

Rethinking God biblically has tremendous potential to reshape our Christian service. The first thing it does is help us to reconsider our view of service itself. In Philippians 2:5–8, Paul pleads with the Christians to cultivate the same mind and attitude that was in Christ Jesus Himself. He gives them Christ's example, reminding them that though He was in the form of God (truly God), He humbled Himself and took on our humanity. This required that He lay aside His glory and enter into our life, taking on a human body and soul. Fully God and fully man, He embraced the work of a servant. Matthew recorded an event that showed how much the disciples needed to be taught Jesus' way of thinking. The mother of James and John came to Christ and asked if her two sons might have positions of honor in the kingdom of God. The Bible says that when the other ten disciples heard it, "They were greatly displeased with the two brothers. But Jesus called them to Himself and said, 'You know that the rulers of the Gentiles lord it over them, and those who are great exercise authority over them. Yet it shall not be so among you; but whoever desires to become great among you, let him be your servant. And whoever desires to be first among you, let him be your slave—just as the Son of Man did not come to be served, but to serve, and to give His life a ransom for many'" (Matthew 20:24–28).

Have you ever stopped and studied the humility of God as it is seen in His Son's work? Have you ever viewed the unique glory of the triune God's humility in the life of Christ? What other religion even pretends that its god is humble? Our God alone possesses the unexpected splendor of humility. Stop and ask yourself this: Have you found humility to be one of the most beautiful attributes of Jesus of Nazareth? Have you come to adore it in such a way that you desire to be like Him, especially in how you serve? Beholding God in His Son's labors will change the way you think about a life of service.

The second thing a biblical view of God will do for our Christian service is change our motivation. Many people might think, "If I give my time and energy to help people, well, who really cares about motivation? All that matters is that people are helped." God cares about motivation. There are several motives that displease God but seem harmless to us. One wrong motivation is desire for praise—either praise we offer ourselves or praise others give us. We probably prefer to call it affirmation. We cannot correctly serve others from this motivation. The pattern of Jesus Christ is so clear on this issue. "[Jesus] came to His own, and His own did not receive Him" (John 1:11). He made the world, then came into the world, and the world He made rejected Him. Surely, in His perfect obedience to God the Father, Jesus should have been recognized as the Son of God by His own family. Instead, His own brothers rejected Him. His own church and pastors were part of the crowd that called for His crucifixion, even after three years of ceaseless service during His public ministry. Even His disciples deserted Him. It is clear that in serving others Jesus did not seek affirmation. He refused to use the service entrusted to Him by His Father to gain affirmation from men. In John 5:41 He said, "I do not receive honor from men." In

John 8:50, again, He says, "I do not seek My own glory." Another time, He explains that only those who don't chase after the praise of their fellow men can be trusted to speak what God gave them to speak (John 7:16–18). How different Christ's humility was from the pride of the Pharisees. In John 5:44, Christ said to the Pharisees, "How can you believe, who receive honor from one another, and do not seek the honor that comes from the only God?" Did you read that carefully? It is impossible for you to believe what Christ taught if you are still craving affirmation from man.

Another wrong motive is performing Christian service to gain a sense of purpose. Some may consider this a perfectly good motive. It is one of the most popular tools to fill a church building: Invite people in and hand them a task to do that gives them a sense of significance and purpose. But if you attract people to your church by making them feel significant, you have made *self*, not God, the reason for all you are doing. It is idolatry to use Christian service to achieve a sense of self-significance. Our personal benefit becomes the ultimate goal of our service.

Still another bad motive is guilt. Who has not been manipulated by guilt to do some act of service? A person might ask you to help with something in the church, but it is done in way that insinuates that you are not a very good Christian if you say no. Even worse, we attempt to remove our guilt before God by trying to use acts of service to appease God, to pay for some of the things we've done wrong. This kind of thinking is ingrained in all of us. We say we are saved by grace, but deep within we are prone to think that sacrificial service will somehow make God love us a little more.

Other wrong motives appear more noble than the ones above. For example, there is the desire to see a person's life changed. While it certainly rises higher than the desire to be affirmed or for our service to others to feed a sense of self-significance, it still falls short of where we need to be. There is also the problem that even when we sacrificially serve others, we are not guaranteed that they will be truly helped. They may absorb all we offer them and still walk toward self-destruction. They may be the object of our energy, emotion, and concern and still not recognize that we are doing what we are doing from love. If your motives are wrong, there is a chance you will become bitter with people and, ultimately, with God. When you pour your life into others through Christian service and they don't appear to be benefitted at all, it is easy to say to God, "If the next person You bring my way is not going to be really helped, don't bother, God. I don't want to waste my time." When you feel that way, you know you have a wrong motivation for your service.

If all of these are wrong motives, then what is the right motive? The right motivation is love. Love to God, and, yes, love to others. What did Christ teach us about love to God? In John 14:15, He says, "If you love Me, you will keep My commandments" (NASB). If we love God, then we will keep His commands. That is Jesus' teaching. So, ultimately, love to God is why we think of others and their needs even above our own. But what is Jesus' example? Consider what we read at the end of that same chapter. Immediately before Jesus leaves the upper room and goes to Gethsemane on the night of his arrest, He says to the disciples, "That the world may know that I love the Father, and as the Father gave Me commandment, so I do. Arise, let us go from here" (John 14:31). Going "from there" meant that Christ was going to the cross. The disciples didn't understand that, but Christ did. The pattern of Christ is this: Even the cross is primarily a God-centered event. Christ gives His life for His church. And yet, He wanted the whole world to know that He did so first and foremost because of the love He had for His Father. It was not just talk. From eternity past, the Father entrusted His Son with a task: to die on the cross as the representative and sin-bearer of His people. To show love to the Father, Christ went to the cross. Amazing! The most humanly beneficial event in the history of the world was rooted in Jesus' love for His Father. By teaching and by example, Jesus shows us that deeds of compassion and mercy for our fellow man begin with love for our God. Beholding God through the obedient service of the Son makes us rethink our motivation for service.

The third thing a biblical view of God changes in our approach to Christian service is our view of who is in charge. One of the differences between well-meaning, sincere humanitarian efforts and Christian service is found in this significant word: initiative. Masters initiate. Servants do not initiate; they implement the master's plans. Let there be no doubt about it—God is the Master in His kingdom, church, family, and creation. God alone has the authority to initiate. Jesus was the servant of His Father. He did not initiate anything in His ministry. He did all things in response to the Father's direction, therefore in harmony with the Father's will. That means the Father chose the way and the timing of Jesus' labors. This distinction is very important. We can do a lot of apparently noble things on our own initiative, but we may be disobeying God all the while. The pattern of Christ requires that we be responsive to God because we are His servants. Jesus said, "My food is to do the will of Him who sent Me, and to finish His work" (John 4:34). Later, He said, "I have come down from heaven, not to do My own will, but the will of Him who sent Me" (John 6:38). The acts of service that Jesus accomplished were guided by the overriding purpose of His earthly life: To do the will of the Father. Helping people, saving His enemies, healing the spiritually diseased—it was all accomplished by following the Father's initiative. Have you ever noticed that Jesus Christ did not do all the good possible to all the people He came across? If that were His goal, how would He have slept? How would He have ever taken the disciples aside for a day of rest and instruction? How would He have ever had a quiet time when the city nearby His place of prayer was full of sick and dying people? Christ was compassionate, but His compassion was guided by the will of the Father.

Now, that brings us back to the issue of initiative, doesn't it? In the Gospel of John, Jesus says, "Most assuredly, I say to you, the Son can do nothing of Himself, but what He sees the Father do; for whatever He does, the Son also does in like manner" (John 5:19). Did you notice that detail? The Son observes and does what the Father does. Christ's activity and methods were an imitation of His Father's activity and methods. Our activity and methods must be an imitation of our Lord, too. We do not act on our own. We are not free to determine what we think is the best way to be effective in kingdom work. We are not in charge of how much we will serve, when we will serve, and for whom we will serve. And yet, self-initiating servants are praised in churches. It isn't that our activity is bad, but if we are in charge, it is not Christian service. "My ministry" is a term Americans use frequently, perhaps more than Christians in other cultures. We like the idea of having the significance of our own personal ministry. But is it Christian service if God did not initiate it? Religious, yes—but Christian?

Another aspect that distinguishes Christ's service from mere acts of human kindness is what He said to people. If we are to follow the pattern of Christ, it is important to notice His words. You probably have taken food to a person who's had a surgery. The family is thankful and say a couple of nice words to you. You only have a few moments to visit, and you want to say the right words to them. What will you say? Those few words have the potential of pointing them to God or to something else. When you visit a person who is in the midst of marital problems and divorce seems inevitable, it is heartbreaking. You listen as a friend tells you about the ten, fifteen, twenty years she's been unhappy. She looks at you at the end of her story waiting for affirmation that she is making the right choice—that she has the right to do what she thinks will make her happy. What do you say? Do you comfort her? Do you encourage? Do you rebuke? Do you plead? How do you know what to say?

How did Christ, our perfect example, know what to say? Christ said, “My doctrine [My teaching] is not Mine, but His who sent Me” (John 7:16). In John 8:26, we read, “I speak to the world those things which I heard from Him.” In John 8:38, Jesus explains, “I speak what I have seen with My Father.” Again, in John 12:50, He says, “Whatever I speak, just as the Father has told Me, so I speak.” Do you see the picture He is drawing? Every day, Jesus woke early and sought solitude with His Father. With the Scriptures open, He listened, He saw, He was taught by His Father. He rose and took the things He learned and applied them to the opportunities of the day. Is that where you get the words you speak to people? Or do you have such a high view of yourself that you feel competent to be a fountain of commonsense and neglect Christ’s pattern? Beholding God in His Son will change the way we speak to those whom we serve.

If we are going to rethink service in the kingdom of God, we will have to realize that every Christian is called to follow *the* Servant, and as such we can’t limit Christian service to Sundays. The pattern of Christ for service is sufficient for every day of the week. In Philippians 2, we see Christ’s true deity. When He takes the form of a servant (humanity), He is a true servant. Jesus is not merely performing a role or wearing a mask. His deity is real. His humanity is real. His servant-status is real. Even now, enthroned in heaven, He still serves His church. He intercedes for her and is ruling over all the worlds alone for her. We cannot do occasional acts of kindness and think that makes us good Christian servants. Acts of kindness are good, but they are not enough to be Christ honoring.

A person can be like a rich businessman who has planned a dinner with coworkers at his home. His wife cleans and cooks all day and puts on this great spread. Everyone eats the amazing meal, completes their friendly meeting, and afterwards the husband puts on an apron. The rest of the family is shocked. He cleans up the dishes, puts them away, and sits down. The visitors are impressed, but the family knows his actions are just for show. There is a difference, isn't there, between what this mom does every day, serving in the home, and what the dad does to impress people? We cannot only act the part of servants when we are on display. The world will see through it.

If we biblically recalibrate our view of what a servant is in light of God, we will aim at something much higher than the temporary relief of human need. It is good to help suffering people. It is Christian to care about the physical and mental health of our fellow man. We don't want to be like the man who is described in the book of James—who has empty religious talk, but when people come to him with real physical needs, gives them religious words and sends them away empty (James 2:14–18). Peter counselled early believers, "Above all things have fervent love for one another, for *'love will cover a multitude of sins.'* Be hospitable to one another without grumbling. As each one has received a gift, minister it to one another, as good stewards of the manifold grace of God. If anyone speaks, *let him speak* as the oracles [words] of God. If anyone ministers, *let him do it* as with the ability which God supplies, that in all things God may be glorified through Jesus Christ, to whom belong the glory and the dominion forever and ever" (1 Peter 4:8–11). That must be our goal too. In other words, our deeds of kindness, in whatever commonplace way we are serving, should leave behind the aroma of Christ. Remember Paul's words to the Ephesian believers: "Therefore be imitators of God as dear children. And walk in love, as Christ also has loved us and given Himself for us, an offering and a sacrifice to God for a sweet-smelling aroma" (Ephesians 5:1). What a picture. We follow Christ, imitating His way of loving God and people. We give of ourselves and by doing so become not only a channel of God's grace to others, but also a sweet-smelling sacrifice to God. Every act of service, done in dependence upon Christ and yielded to His pattern, ought to fill the lives of people around us with the perfume of Christ. They may see you serving, but they are smelling Christ.

A real-life example of this type of servanthood can be found in the life of Hudson Taylor, a missionary to China. Taylor's ministry encouraged over a thousand missionaries to join him in inland China. By all contemporary accounts, he was not an outwardly impressive man. When he got up to speak at conferences, people were often disappointed at first sight. He was neither an amazing orator nor a brilliant writer. So, what was so significant about Hudson Taylor that encouraged so many people to go to China, trusting his leadership? After his death, one of his friends wrote, "I lived with Hudson Taylor a long time. I watched him. That was a life that bore looking into."[3] What was so impressive about Hudson Taylor was not his great gifts; it was his great Christlikeness, viewed in the context of a lifetime of serving in China through medical missions and preaching. At one point, Taylor traveled through China as a missionary with a group of younger men, one of whom was C. T. Studd. These twenty-year-old men thought that they could keep up with Hudson Taylor who was in his fifties. He had a weak constitution and was sick a lot, but he was accustomed to the missionary life. The group was travelling from south China to the north. They were going through mountains and spent fourteen to sixteen hours a day walking. Every morning, as the younger men woke up, they found that Hudson Taylor was already awake and breakfast was made. He woke himself hours before dawn to read his Bible by candlelight. After this time alone with God, he made breakfast before waking the younger men.

Still later in life, Taylor travelled through the United States and Europe. He and other leaders spent the night at a Christian's home. At that time in history, hotel services took dirty shoes that had been placed outside the doors and cleaned and polished them while the guests slept. While staying in this Christian's home, Hudson Taylor got up long before dawn, met with the Lord, then quietly went from room to room throughout the house, gathering all the other men's shoes. He then cleaned and polished them and put them at their doors. He was always quietly serving: Hudson Taylor's life was a life that bore looking into. Every opportunity we take to do good to someone has the potential to be an event that unveils the greatness and the goodness of God. Every act of service, in some small way, can leave behind the lingering aroma of the living God.

[1] Mark A. Noll, *America's God: From Jonathan Edwards to Abraham Lincoln* (United Kingdom: Oxford University Press, 2002), 191.
[2] Robert Murray M'Cheyne, *Memoir and Remains of the Rev. Robert Murray M'Cheyne*, ed. Andrew A. Bonar (Edinburgh: Banner of Truth, 1844/1966), 282.
[3] Dr. & Mrs. Howard Taylor, *Hudson Taylor and The China Inland Mission: The Growth of a Work of God* (Overseas Mission Fellowship: Singapore, 1919/1988,1989), 414–416.

If we insist on trying to imagine Him, we end with an idol, made not with the hands, but with thoughts; and an idol of the mind is as offensive to God as an idol of the hand.[1]

A.W. TOZER

10

BEHOLDING GOD

Beholding a Lesser God?

In the 1950s, A. W. Tozer watched the explosive growth of the American evangelical church with concern over symptoms that were emerging. He wrote in *The Knowledge of the Holy*, "This generation of churchgoers has not seen the glory of God. The god that they are acquainted with is hardly better than that of the Romans and the Greeks, if he is not, in fact, less than them."[2] If I might borrow the title of a movie from the 1980s, I think we can say that the American churches have, in great measure, become "*Children of a Lesser God*." One symptom of this is that what we know of God's greatness is largely drawn from what we have read of church history or the Scriptures. We don't really expect to see God's mighty works in our day. We try changing the externals and hope the next church program, like a new paint job, will fix the trouble within the church. One thing is undeniably true: If the churches in America continue their current trajectory and simply put greater effort, energy, time, and money into achieving numerical success, in ten years we will be worse off than we are today. We will have promoted a wider spread of idolatry. We will not have promoted the worship of the biblical God. One of the most detrimental things we can do is the thing we are most tempted to do—to pick up the pace and run harder in a wrong direction.

If merely increasing our current efforts is not the answer, what should the church do? We should go back to that foundational question: "Who are you, God?" We should rethink everything based on the biblical answer to that question. We want to be guided by His Word, so we open our Bibles and we lay all we do before that all-authoritative, all-sufficient Book. We take what we believe, our ministerial philosophy, our programs, every activity and event in the life of the church and lay them before the Lord. But to be biblically guided means more than mimicking what we see in the Bible and following God's commands for laboring in His kingdom. It must include doing all of that for *love* of the King! Too much of what passes for Christianity on an average Sunday morning is nothing more than a subtle form of idol worship. This statement, of course, does not apply to every gathering on Sundays. It is also a strong statement that requires more explanation. To understand this assessment of American Christianity, we first need a clearer understanding of the nature of idolatry. We need to understand what it is that lies at the root of idolatry, no matter what form it takes or what time in history it occurs. Secondly, we will need to unmask the popular ways that an idolatrously low view of God manifests itself in a church. Finally, we will consider the costs that we can expect to pay if we are unwilling to bring our understanding of God back in line with what we find in the Bible.

Let's begin by coming to grips with the nature of idolatry itself. Ancient idols might be easy to spot, but what does an idol look like in modern clothing? Idols are at home in any century, any country, any home, even any religious gathering. They can be adapted to the seeker-friendly church as well as the staunchly Reformed gathering. They can appeal to those who are centered on emotions, on

Christian activism, or on doctrinal precision. We find, as we read the Bible from Genesis to Revelation, that idolatry is a problem that plagues all mankind. Paul warned the Colossian church against the expressions of moral impurity that were common in their day. He ends the list with greed, or covetousness, and notes that this particular sin is equivalent to "idolatry" (Colossians 3:5). In his first letter, John writes, "Little children, keep yourselves from idols" (1 John 5:21). In the book, *No God but God*, we find helpful and searching descriptions of idolatry: "Idols are nonexistent. They are mere fictions. They are false gods. But this knowledge by itself is not a safeguard against idolatry. There is no defense against idolatry in abstract biblical truth alone."[3] It is easy to admit that human ideas of God—gods that don't not exist outside of our imaginations—are idols. We agree that there is no other god but God. Yet acknowledging that idols are not real gods does not stop our hearts from drifting toward idolatry.

Let's consider five characteristics that are true of all idols, in the hope that we might become better at spotting idolatry in ourselves. First, idols come in many forms. Idols may take obvious, typical forms. These may have both the wrong name for God and the wrong form. Examples of this type of idol include Hindu gods as well as Baal and Molech—ancient idols frequently mentioned in the Old Testament. These idols are obvious, easily discerned, and not likely to tempt modern Christians. However, there are more subtle forms of idolatry. These may bear the right name for God but the wrong form. One well-known example of this type of idol is the golden calf in the book of Exodus. There is much for us to learn from this particular example. The nation of Israel was brought out of Egyptian bondage through an extraordinary display of God's power. Once Israel was safely out of Egypt, Moses was called by God to go up a mountain alone to meet with the Lord. He was gone for quite some time. The Jews, who lived surrounded by Egyptian idols for centuries, were now in a wilderness, learning to worship an invisible God. This was something they apparently weren't comfortable with, so they asked Aaron and the leaders to make them a god. They weren't sure what happened to Moses. Sadly, Aaron took earrings from the people and fashioned a golden calf. The leaders told the people, "This is your god, O Israel, that brought you out of the land of Egypt" (Exodus 32:4). Notice they did not try to add a new cow-god to the worship of the Lord. They simply built an idol and called it "The god that brought you out of Egypt" (Exodus 32:4). Aaron told the people to prepare themselves that day because the next day they were going to have a feast to the LORD (Exodus 32:5). Aaron was a monotheist. He is telling them that they only have one God, but he is putting the true God in a new form. Thus, they used the right name for God, but they adjusted His form. When we adjust God to fit our appetites, our desires, and our culture, but keep the name *Jesus*, we have crafted an idol in our hearts—in our churches—just as surely as Aaron carved a golden calf.

We need to face a difficult fact about idolatry. The most productive idol factory in human history is not located in Egypt, China, or Africa. It is in the human heart. Tozer warned us, "Left to ourselves, we tend immediately to reduce God to manageable terms. We want to get Him where we can use Him or at least know where He is when we need Him."[4] Manageable. Useful. Available. That is the god humanity prefers. Whether we have an obvious idol carved out of stone or whether we have a subtle idol—an adjusted Jesus that is crafted in our imaginations—an idol is always something that we embrace as a substitute for the living God.

Second, idols not only promise what God alone can give but also promise these things at half the price. They promise to do noble things for you, such as rescuing your marriage, making your children interested in Christianity, or getting your finances under control. Of course, idols promise these benefits in a way that requires you to compromise. You will have to say *no* to the real God in order to say *yes* to the idol. These idols promise what God alone can give, but they always, always lie. They lie about themselves and they lie about what they can do. The Old Testament often repeats this fact in words like the following: "Idols…have mouths, but they do not speak; eyes they have, but they do not see; they have ears, but they do not hear; noses they have, but they do not smell; they have hands, but they do not handle; feet they have, but they do not walk; nor do they mutter through their throat" (Psalm 115:5–7). The common trait of all idols, ancient and modern, is this: When you put your hope in gods that don't exist, you discover that they can never actually do anything for you. The Jesus of the American imagination can't do anything for you, either. He doesn't exist.

Third, idols are essentially a way to maintain your religion with a new center—a new beneficiary. All idolatry involves a deep self-centeredness. You want to be promoted, fulfilled, satisfied, and affirmed, so you craft a counterfeit god in your mind that will tolerate a religion with you at the center. Only a counterfeit Jesus is satisfied when you are at the center of your Sunday worship and rule your Monday through Saturdays, while you continue to read your Bible and say your prayers. Any religion where Jesus orbits you—exists for you—is built on a counterfeit version of the true God.

Fourth, idols always take the form of the surrounding cultural gods. We may never be tempted to make a Hindu statue to worship, but we will be tempted to make idols that reflect the culture of our nation or region. For example, entertainment is an idol of the American culture. It promises so much, doesn't it? It promises us happiness, peace, and a temporary escape from sorrow or emptiness. So, we add it to our worship services in order to attract those who are not attracted by God. We give the worship service over to pop music, expressive dance, drama, even movie clips that form the heart of a moral chat. When it comes to prayer, well, prayer is often nonexistent except to open and close the meeting. Is this the kind of worship that the early New Testament church would recognize as Christian?

Fifth, idols enter the life when room is made for them through failure to seek the living God. It has been said, "When we cease to worship God, we do not worship nothing. We worship anything."[5] Where there is a neglect of real, earnest, heartfelt focus upon the person of God, an idol will always fill the gap. In this area, as in so many others, a good offense is the best defense.

It is also important to recognize other ways that inadequate views of God affect our lives. I want to mention two of these that we may not have thought of: practical atheism and practical deism.[6] Practical atheism occurs when we claim to believe that God exists, but we live as if He either *is not*, or as if *He is other than* what He describes Himself to be. Have you ever asked how our lifestyles would change if God was not as He is described in the Bible? Would we make choices differently? Would we eat differently, dress differently, listen to different music, flip through the channels on our television differently? Would we respond differently to our spouse and children? Would we approach our work differently? If God ceased to be, would your coworkers and family members notice a great difference in the way you lived throughout the week? We might confidently answer, "Yes!" But let's put the question another way: How exactly are your practical choices affected by the fact that He is as He's described Himself to be? Can you think of any direct cause and effect connection between a passage in the Bible that you recently studied, in which you found your God described, and an area of your life that was adjusted in light of that description? Being a practical atheist allows you to maintain all your orthodox statements about God; it simply doesn't lead you to live them out practically.

Not only does an idolatrously low view of God show itself in practical atheism, but it also shows up as practical deism. Deism is a word that we do not often use, but it was a hotly debated topic in the eighteenth century churches in Britain and America. Deism allows for belief in a wise, powerful, transcendent being who created all things. But after creating, the god of the deist steps back from his creation, leaving it to function by a set of natural laws. It was an attempt to stem the tide of unbelief that swept across much of Europe in the early eighteenth century. Deism was intended to make room for God—only a god that was adjusted to the ideals of the eighteenth century thinkers, so much so that he hardly resembled the God of the Bible. When a deist encountered biblical accounts of miracles, he said, "That cannot be true. That must have been added by the adherents of Christianity years after the life of Jesus." Deism accepted the idea of a creator, but this creator did not meddle in human affairs. Of course, that meant that key events like the incarnation, death, and resurrection of God's Son, to the deist, were simply fictional stories. For the deist, God never invades the here and now, nor does He intervene in human history.

Why don't we have deist churches on every corner in American and British cities today? Deism could not survive the reality of the Great Awakening. It became impossible to hold to the idea that God doesn't intervene in human history in light of the lives being changed by the preaching of men like George Whitefield, John Wesley, and Jonathan Edwards.

Sadly, a practical deism still survives today. It is alive and well in churches and Christian schools. It thrives in both conservative and liberal churches. Practical deism accepts any biblical statement about God as truth, but it leads us to live as if the God of the Bible does not interfere with our lives in the here and now. We see practical deism in churches: People are busy trying to do good for the souls of those around them. Bible phrases are still used. But when you look beneath the surface, the church no longer expects God to actually do anything. So it is left up to the church to fix people.

When a church has more committee meetings than prayer meetings, it might be a deistic church—at least in practice. Practical deism sees no reason to wrestle with God in prayer. He's there, He's holy, He's glorious, but He doesn't interfere. He's not going to do anything. Based on that logic, prayer meetings are useless—a waste of valuable time. Even tedious committee meetings have some worth because these accomplish something. Practical deism is death to practical Christianity. Every biblical description of God is withered by the touch of practical deism, because one must conclude that those sublime passages are not meant for real life, here and now. Practical atheism and practical deism are common ways that an idolatrous view of God reveals itself.

Finally, you need to consider the costs both of returning to a biblical view of God and of failing to do so. Letting God define Himself may turn your life upside down. Churches, families, workplaces—everything will be affected. There will be those reading this sermon who will pay this high cost, and they will experience a Christianity that is more than a mere notion. There will be others who come to the edge of the truth about God, look over the precipice, and turn back in unbelief. You must count the cost involved in rethinking God biblically. But there is another cost that needs to be measured. There is a bitter, enduring cost of willfully maintaining low and unbiblical views of God. Remember, God does not reward the devotion offered to false gods who borrow His name. The god of your imagination may resemble aspects of the real God, but God will not be pleased with your idolatrous creation. Perhaps a simple illustration will help here: Imagine a man comes home to find an imposter in his house. The imposter is sitting at the man's table with his kids and his wife. He's wearing the man's clothes. He looks like the man and he even has the same name. The family sees the true husband and father come in and they say, "Oh, it's a little awkward, but we've replaced you. We don't really like living with you. However, there are a lot of things about you that we do like, so we decided to replace you with someone very similar." Would that man be flattered? When God sees your church service this Sunday, will He find an imposter bearing the name of His Son, looking and sounding similar to His Son, at the center of your worship? If you worship a Jesus you invented, will God be flattered?

Have you ever considered the cost of an entire life of religious devotion burned up and rejected at the judgment seat of Christ because you offered your life to a god that doesn't even exist? We come to God and say, "What about the prayers, the Bible studies, the gifts, the time spent in church activities? What about all the things I wouldn't do and all the ways I denied myself?" What if God should respond, "You *did not* do it unto Me" (Matthew 25:40)? This is a frightening reality: God will not accept idolatrous worship offered to a counterfeit version of Himself in a church this Sunday any more than He accepted the worship offered to the golden calf in the wilderness.

Malachi addressed the Jews of his day, who allowed low views of God to creep into their worship. They were happy to give God sick and lame sheep from their flocks for the sacrifice. God said to the people through the prophet, "Who is there even among you who would shut the doors, so that you would not kindle fire on My altar in vain? I have no pleasure in you...nor will I accept an offering from your hands" (Malachi 1:10). Is God pleased that your church's doors are still open? We certainly desire that God would find pleasure in our prayers, songs, and sermons. How can we be sure that He does? We go back to the Bible and plead with God, "Do not allow me to embrace an idol and call it Christ. God, I want to know You as You really are and for that truth to shape every facet of my life. I do not want to be one of the children of the lesser god. You are the only God for me. Teach me."

[1] A .W. Tozer, *The Knowledge of the Holy* (New York: Harper Collins Publishers, 1961), 8.
[2] Ibid.
[3] Os Guinness and John Steel, eds., *No God But God: Breaking with the Idols of Our Age* (Chicago: Moody, 1992), 16.
[4] Tozer, *The Knowledge of the Holy,* 8.
[5] This maxim is widely attributed to G. K. Chesterton though not found in this form in his works.
[6] Stephen Charnock, *The Complete Works of Stephen Charnock* (United Kingdom: James Nichol, 1864), 185.

We trust Him whose power will never be exhausted, whose love will never wane, whose kindness will never change, whose faithfulness will never fail, whose wisdom will never be nonplussed, and whose perfect goodness can never know a diminution!

C.H. SPURGEON

11

BEHOLDING GOD

Avoiding the Lies of Pragmatism

Amy Carmichael (1867–1951) was a single woman who served for over fifty years without furlough as a missionary in India. She led a mission that took in rescued children from temple prostitution in the Hindu system. The missionaries had to deal with the countless daily needs of raising these children, and as head of the mission, Amy navigated these uncharted waters in the midst of a hostile culture. Though she often prayed that God would bring a man who could carry the burden of directing this mission, none was provided. How did she endure for fifty years? During a particularly difficult season in the mission, Amy went alone to the seaside to think and pray. She asked God, "Will You be enough for this life?" As she sat there, she watched the tide come in and the waves sweep across the sand. The little shells along the shore were filled with the seawater and she realized that God, being a shoreless ocean of grace, would never fail to fill the little seashell life of a missionary.[1] Her mission went on to demonstrate the truth of God's faithfulness. Like Amy Carmichael, we must take the truths we are learning about our God and apply them in the various crisis moments that we will face. It is not easy to trust God when faced with the unrelenting march of human need and our own inadequacy. But it is right.

Those who are determined to press on in knowing the Lord need to be prepared for a coming crisis. This crisis *will* come. There is always a crisis when we are confronted by the realities of God in the Bible because a response is always required on our part. There is a crisis because of the cost of obedience. When we are faced with a high cost of obedience, the question becomes, "Do you really believe God?" How do we answer that type of question? The choice we make next proves whether we believe God or not. Too often, when the truth of God meets our real-life situations and we must make a choice, disobedience is the result. Disobedience can be summed up in the little phrase, "Yes, Lord, but..." We acknowledge a certain truth about God, and we see that it has application to the present situation, but instead of living on that truth, we respond with "Yes, Lord, but…" It is not an exaggeration to claim that throughout much of Western evangelicalism, we are witnessing a widespread betrayal of Jesus in His own church, covered with the innocent sounding phrase, "Yes, Lord, but..."

The root of "Yes, Lord, but..." is unbelief. Unbelief grows in the soil of a life that harbors small, unbiblical views of God. It grows in the life that knows God only by what it has heard from others. Unbelief is the root and spiritual cowardice is the fruit. God includes spiritual cowards in a list of those who will inhabit hell. Revelation 21:8 states, "…the cowardly, unbelieving, abominable, murderers, sexually immoral, sorcerers, idolaters, and all liars shall have their part in the lake which burns with fire and brimstone, which is the second death." Spiritual cowardice will land a person in hell just as surely as unbelief or murder or any other heinous sin. In our day, instead of labeling someone a spiritual coward, we would call a person who says, "Yes, Lord, but...," a spiritual pragmatist. They may even be praised for being practical, sensible people.

Pragmatism is often a cover for rebellion. Pragmatism is a perspective which values an idea, concept, belief, program, or course of action for its apparent effectiveness. Pragmatism believes that if something works, it must be right. Because pragmatism values something for its effectiveness, as soon as it stops being effective it is discarded. An illustration of pragmatism is as follows: A person is floating in the sea after a shipwreck. There are no lifeboats, and though the distant lights of the shore can be seen, he is never going to reach the shore by swimming. His strength is spent. He is going under and believes he has no hope until a piece of wood floats by. He is so excited! He grabs it, and by using the wood to keep himself afloat, he slowly makes his way to the safety of the shore. When he gets to shore, he does not carry this piece of wood around with him the rest of his life, clinging to it. He loved it while it was useful, but now that he is on shore, he has no use for it and tosses it aside.

That is how pragmatism treats biblical truths. When a certain passage of Scripture appears useful for fixing our marriages, our families, or our churches, we cling to it. As soon as something else looks like it's going to be more helpful, we leave Scripture behind. Pragmatism does not value truth because it's true; it values truth only if it is (apparently) effective. Many who claim to follow Christ base their life on pragmatism. They never ask the question, "Are my choices guided by the clearest teachings of Scripture?" Instead, they ask, "Is this going to work?"

Spiritual pragmatism is prevalent in churches. When they are faced with the need to attract young people to church, many churches turn to what they think will work, rather than looking to the biblical pattern. The youth committee gets together and looks at several options. A plan is chosen because it appears to have worked for other churches. No one on the committee stops to ask, "Is this the most Christ-like manner of reaching young people? Is this approach based on the biblical teaching of God's character and ways?"

Instead, the question will be, "Will it work here like it worked other places?"

Consider how pragmatism might impact the family. You study the Scripture and desire to apply what you are learning about God. Your family may not in agreement with these new ideas. Obedience to God in rethinking family choices may cause strife within your home. You want the young adults in your home to enjoy going to church, and you want them to keep going to church when they leave your home, so you are tempted to pick a church based on their desires—their appetites. For example, if your child plays drums and Church A doesn't have drums but Church B, a church that is not careful in what it teaches, does have drums, you will go to Church B. You choose church B, even though you acknowledge that church B is not faithfully handling the truth. The root of this choice is spiritual pragmatism. You don't trust God enough to obey Him regardless of what your children think.

Many Christians can look back to a time in their life when they launched out in faith upon God. They really depended upon Him, they cried out to Him, they trusted Him, but their plans never were realized. Now they say, "God didn't work for me." The truth is, many of them put their faith in a god that does not exist. This is not the God of the Bible. They hoped and trusted that God would do something which He has stated in Scripture that He will not do. Knowing the character of God, pursuing the clearest views of Him and applying it to every area in life, will teach us who He is. We must ask ourselves a question: Are we really trusting the God of the Bible? Are we asking Him to do what He said He will do, or have we invented a false god who will do whatever we ask?

Whether it is an individual, a family, a church, or a denomination, when we open the Bible and are confronted with God, we must decide: "Now what am I going to do?" This crisis is particularly pronounced in the life of a leader because your decisions are going to affect not only yourself, but other people whom you serve. The Bible gives us examples, both good and bad, of those who either embraced pragmatism or refused to do so and trusted God. Three examples from Scripture demonstrate the different effects of spiritual pragmatism. The first is an example of pragmatic disobedience that ended in utter destruction. The second is an example of pragmatic disobedience that ended in repentance and life, and the third is an example of obedience (the refusal of spiritual pragmatism) that resulted in life for many.

The first example of pragmatism can be seen in the life of a man named Jeroboam. In this Old Testament scene, Solomon, the king, is old. His heart has gone after the idols of his many wives. God is offended by Solomon's idolatry, and He takes ten of the tribes away from the house of David. Solomon's son, Rehoboam, will still have a kingdom, but it will be very small. God gives another man the ten northern tribes. Two nations result: Israel to the north, and Judah to the south. Jeroboam was approached by a prophet of God and the prophet tells him that he is the man God has chosen to lead the ten northern tribes. God tells Jeroboam that if he will set his heart toward God, trust Him, follow Him, and obey Him, then Jeroboam will receive the promises given to King David. When Jeroboam becomes king of the northern ten tribes, he immediately proves that he doubts God. His unbelief produces spiritual cowardice which results in several very practical, very sensible sounding, but very ungodly decisions.

Instead of trusting God, Jeroboam began to worry that if the ten northern tribes continued to go down to Jerusalem for special seasons of worship at the temple, their hearts would soften toward the Davidic line. If these northern tribes decided to reunite with the southern kingdom, Jeroboam would be removed and killed as a usurper. He decides to build two rival worship sites for the northern tribes, replacing the temple in Jerusalem (located in the newly formed southern nation of Judah), which God had designated as the proper place for this worship. These new worship sites would have four apparent advantages: worship would be more convenient, priests would not have to meet biblical standards, the same worship practices could be used as were used in Jerusalem, and by building two golden calves, the people would have a form of God they preferred.[2]

The result of this spiritual pragmatism was nothing like what Jeroboam envisioned. God judges Jeroboam. He and his entire family, all his descendants, were wiped out. God handed them over to their enemies. Israel, embracing this idolatry, refused to listen to the prophets whom God sent them, generation after generation. God handed them over to the Assyrians to be disciplined. God makes it very clear: "Then Jeroboam drove Israel from following the LORD and made them commit a great sin. For the children of Israel walked in all the sins of Jeroboam which he did; they did not depart from them, until the LORD removed Israel out of His sight, as He had said by all His servants the prophets. So Israel was carried away from their own land to Assyria, *as it is* to this day" (2 Kings 17:21–23).

Would you be surprised to hear that the sin of Jeroboam is alive and well in churches today? We are told that people won't attend church if it is inconvenient, so we redesign the activities of the church with convenience in mind. We have handed the church to Jeroboam. We are told that restricting those who can serve in leadership positions will result in the loss of members, so we allow anyone to be a leader whether they are biblically qualified or not. How many small churches have men in leadership positions because they are the men of wealth and influence in the community, not because they possess the biblical qualifications? We have handed the church to Jeroboam. There are also golden calves—surely, we don't know any churches with those! But do we adjust God, like Jeroboam did, to conform to the appetites of the people? One of the most numerically successful churches in America, when the church was still in the planning stages and not yet established, sent out thousands of questionnaires asking the people in the neighboring communities to give a description of the kind of church they would want in their community. The religious strategists tabulated the responses and crafted a church according to the appetite of the people. Another way of describing this clever approach is this: They handed the church to Jeroboam. All that is required to be like Jeroboam is an ignorance of God—a doubt that He is enough. Then, marketing strategies appear more sensible, practical, and effective than prayer and Scripture. The result is the same in every generation: We are handing the church to Jeroboam. Remember the outcome for Israel. Generation after generation, hundreds of thousands of Jews grew up under that idolatrous system, started by Jeroboam and propagated by compromised priests. Those Jews will populate hell forever because they trusted their leaders and devoted themselves to idols. At the time, it all must have seemed so clever and modern. As we look back, it seems only tragically unnecessary.

There are other examples of pragmatism that aren't as shocking. Consider the misguided choices of David. When David was settled as king, he wanted to bring the Ark of the Covenant into the center of national life. It was a good desire. The problem was, instead of following God's specific instructions for transporting the Ark, David chose a very sensible sounding alternative. The Levites were supposed to carry the Ark with the gold-plated poles. David put the Ark of the Covenant onto a cart and had oxen pull it. It was a lot faster and easier to pull it on a cart than to find a group of Levites who were willing to carry the Ark to the capital city. While on the journey, the cart hit a rough spot and the Ark was in danger of falling to the ground. A man named Uzzah stretched out his hand to steady it. God then stretched out His hand and struck Uzzah dead. Touching the Ark was forbidden. [3]

Where did David get the idea to use a cart? When the Philistines captured the Ark of the Covenant years prior to this, God cursed them for holding His Ark. The curses were so severe that the Philistines decided to send the Ark back to Israel. The Philistines knew nothing of God's law. They put the Ark on an ox cart and sent it back to Israel.[4] David simply adapted the Philistine method to fit his needs. God refused this adaptation and it cost Uzzah his life. Later, David repents and again attempts to move the Ark, but this time he goes back to the Old Testament laws. He chooses both the people and the method God mandated in Scripture.[5] David's repentance and obedience here were just a foretaste of his godly rule that was at the heart of a spiritual golden era for Israel.

Is there anything like David's Philistine-oriented pragmatism in the church today? How often do we desire to accomplish something spiritually good and search for ideas for how to do so? We surf the internet in hopes of finding someone who devised an effective method that we can use for our own purposes. We hear that a church used a new method with great results, and we want those results. We do not even think to ask, "Is this God's method, according to Scripture? Will these actions please our God?" It would seem that David's pragmatism is alive and well in our churches. The denominations have hired the modern Philistines, secular strategists, to explain how to attract, keep, and manage people. As a result of failing to look at Scripture, we are desperate to find someone with a scheme that will get results. We have handed the church over to strategists, and their marketing techniques are embraced without question.

The good news is that if we recognize these patterns in ourselves, we do not have to continue in them. We do not have to continue to grow our churches by the sins of Jeroboam or accomplish kingdom work with the techniques of the Philistines. Like David, we can come back to the God of the Bible. We can repent of the pride that ignored God's desires. We can actually follow Him. What was the difference between David and Jeroboam? They had many similarities, after all. They were both handpicked by God. They were both given a great task. They were both carrying the honor of God's name as they went about those tasks. They were both rebuked by God for their pragmatism in the early stages of their rule. The main difference is this: One of them repented and one did not. One of them knew God.

Great help is found in the one example of a perfect service: the labors of Jesus Christ. At the beginning of His ministry, Christ was baptized by John. The great labor of redemption was beginning in the public ministry of Christ. The Holy Spirit led Christ into isolation in the wilderness to be tested and tempted for forty days. These tests answered a very important question: "Is Christ trustworthy with this task or will He pick a more practical, seemingly sensible way of accomplishing the salvation of our souls?"

First, Satan tempted Christ by saying, in essence, "Is it necessary for You to be so hungry, Jesus? Why not command these stones to turn to bread?" Jesus refused to turn the stones into bread. Why did He refuse? Because Christ knew the Father and He trusted the Father's timing. Christ knew that when it was time for Him to eat, the Father would provide. Next, Satan implies, "Don't You think it would promote Your message more if You jumped off the tower of the temple and God's angels rescued You? Everyone will know that You are somebody special. You will immediately have the ear of the nation." Again, Christ refused. He refused to follow any road to success but that which was laid out by His Father. Finally, Satan asks Christ to fall down and worship Him, essentially saying, "After all, isn't one secret, isolated act of compromise worth it to save the whole world?" Again, the answer is "No." Jesus Christ knew the Father, and He was not tempted by any of the shortcuts.[6]

Jesus, the most effective Servant-King, was not a pragmatist. He did not hand over the Father's honor by choosing a Jeroboam-like leadership. He did not follow the Philistine strategists of His day. The result was a life and death that appeared, on the surface, to be amazingly ineffective—a waste! The lost world sees that Christ waited thirty years, and then ministered only three, allowing Himself to be captured and put to death. The pragmatic minds of the world cannot see that His was the most effective life ever. No wonder the writer of Hebrews tells us, "Therefore, holy brethren...consider the Apostle and High Priest of our confession, Christ Jesus, who was faithful to Him who appointed Him" (Hebrews 3:1–2).

The subtle pragmatism of "Yes, Lord, but…" sounds innocent, but it destroyed the nation of Israel. It almost destroyed David's early attempts to bring the worship of God into the heart of the nation's capital. More importantly, these words were never uttered by Jesus. Pragmatism still destroys all hope of God being honored in our lives or our churches. It destroys all hope of really helping people. Will we be willing to count the cost of rethinking God biblically and applying what we see to our lives without spiritual cowardice? Will we follow our Lord in rejecting pragmatism's empty promises of effectiveness? Will we choose Christ's path? It is described in the words of Thomas Ragland, an early missionary to India: "Of all plans of ensuring success, the most certain is Christ's own becoming a corn of wheat and falling into the ground and dying. Christ said, 'Truly, truly I say to you, unless a corn of wheat falls into the ground and dies, it remains alone, but if it dies, it brings forth much fruit.'"[7] That is the path for us.

[1] Amy Carmichael, *Toward Jerusalem* (London: Society for Promoting Christian Knowledge, 1937), 68.
Amy Carmichael, *Thou Givest... They Gather* (Fort Washington, PA: Christian Literature Crusade), 1958), 74.
[2] For the full account of Jeroboam's sad life see 1 & 2 Kings and 2 Chronicles. The sins of Jeroboam are mentioned in 1 Kings 14:9.
[3] 2 Samuel 6
[4] 1 Samuel 6
[5] 2 Samuel 6
[6] Matthew 4
[7] Amy Carmichael, *Gold Cord: The Story of a Fellowship* (United States: CLC Publications, 2002), 8.

We cannot organize revival, but we can set our sails to catch the winds of heaven.

G. CAMPBELL MORGAN

12

BEHOLDING GOD

Seeking His Nearness

At the end of the eighteenth century, John Wesley, the cofounder of English Methodism, lay dying. His friends surrounded his bed, whispering back and forth, encouraging each other with tales of the great deeds God had accomplished in that century of revival and how so much of it was accomplished through John Wesley. Wesley stirred himself when he heard his friends say these things and said, "The best of all is, God is with us."[1] In this statement, Wesley was not talking about the great crowds or the excitement. He was making a very important observation. At the heart of the work of the evangelical revival in Britain was the extraordinary nearness of the living God. Amy Carmichael, a century after Wesley, was laboring in the difficult spiritual climate of Hindu India. She said to her weary coworkers, "All we need, all we want is God's ungrieved presence with us always."[2] As a follower of Christ, can you say the same? Is the nearness of God our hearts' desire and greatest need? Is it the desire of our local churches? The church is the steward of the truth about God. We are not to be safety deposit boxes that keep the treasure carefully locked away. Though we want to be careful with the truths about God, to remove any imposters fashioned in our imaginations, there is more to this knowledge than doctrinal precision. Rethinking God ought to include the experiential and relational aspects of His nearness. We want the nearness of God in a way we have not known, and we want to bring others near to Him. God Himself is our goal.

Does it ever bother you when you think of God? There are times when it ought to. It bothered the psalmist, Asaph. In Psalm 77:3–13, he expresses his troubled heart, "I remembered God, and was troubled…I have considered the days of old, the years of ancient times…Will the Lord cast off forever? And will He be favorable no more? Has His mercy ceased forever? Has *His* promise failed forevermore? Has God forgotten to be gracious? Has He in anger shut up His tender mercies? And I said, 'This is my anguish; *but I will remember* the years of the right hand of the Most High. I will remember the works of the Lord…Your way, O God, is in the sanctuary; who *is* so great a god as *our* God?" As you rethink God, you are confronted by passages that describe Him in all His majesty but then look at the poor level of Christian living that you might consider as normal. How can you not be bothered by the contrast? There are times when growing in your knowledge of the God of the Bible leads to the same questions that bothered Asaph.

Are we filled with a longing for God that goes beyond basic biblical facts? The psalmists certainly were. Psalm 42:1 states, "As the deer pants for the water brooks, so pants my soul for You, O God. My soul thirsts for God, for the living God." Psalm 63:1 echoes that longing, "O God, You are my God; early will I seek You; my soul thirsts for You; my flesh longs for You in a dry and thirsty land where there is no water." Asaph says in Psalm 73:25 and 27, "Whom have I in heaven *but You*? And besides You, I desire nothing on earth…For, behold, those who are far from You will perish…But as for me, the nearness of God is my good."[3] We do not want to stop with good beliefs or better behavior. Our aim is to know a Person. Daily communion, fellowship, and intimacy with the God of the Bible is the goal.

When we speak of the experiential aspects of knowing God, there are always those in the church who object. Those objections might sound something like the following: "Is it right to desire more than what God has already provided? You deserved hell, but instead, He has given you pardon. He has granted you adoption into His family. He's given you the promise of heaven. Isn't it a bit childish to say to God, 'Thank you for all these things, but I want more. I want to know the nearness of the living God?'" Others object by asking, "Isn't this talk about experiencing God's nearness in our daily lives going against God's command to live by faith and not by sight?" The answer to these objections is found in Scripture. What God says in His Word must guide the believer's expectations of the Christian life. In His Word, we find that the new covenant provides for the experiential nearness of God in the life of the believer in ways that had not been available to believers in the old covenant.

Where do we find God's nearness explained? Psalm 68:18 prophesies, "You have ascended on high, You have led captivity captive; You have received gifts among men, even *from* the rebellious, that the LORD God might dwell there." This passage in the Psalms refers to the Ark of the Covenant ascending to the temple, and it also points forward to the greater deed of the ascension of Christ. In His ascension, Jesus led our captivity captive. He received gifts. But what is the ultimate result? It is God dwelling among His people. This new covenant privilege is applied by Paul in 2 Corinthians 6:16–7:1, where he deals with a compromised church and attempts to motivate them to repentance. He shows them the relationship between their ethical choices and enjoying, or forfeiting, the nearness of God. He writes, "You are the temple of the living God. As God has said: 'I will dwell in them and will walk among them. I will be their God, and they shall be My people.' Therefore 'Come out from among them and be separate, says the Lord. Do not touch what is unclean and I will receive you. I will be a Father to you, and you shall be My sons and daughters,' says the Lord Almighty. Therefore, having these promises, beloved, let us cleanse ourselves from all filthiness of the flesh and spirit, perfecting holiness in the fear of God." Paul gathered all those Old Testament promises and tells the New Testament Christians that, because of the finished work of Christ, these promises are for them. Paul exhorts them to quit toying around with the filth of sin, sins of the flesh, the heart, and the mind. Christians have been promised God, dwelling with and walking among His people. Or, consider what James says in James 4. In order to draw an adulterous-hearted church away from love of the world, he writes, "Adulterers and adulteresses! Do you not know that friendship with the world is enmity with God? Whoever therefore wants to be a friend of the world makes himself an enemy of God . . . Draw near to God and He will draw near to you" (James 4:4,8).

In another passage, Paul prays for the Ephesian church. These Ephesians are already Christians, and yet Paul prays that God would fill them with His fullness. Paul prayed, "That Christ may dwell in your hearts through faith; that you, being rooted and grounded in love, may be able to comprehend with all the saints what is the width and length and depth and height—to know the love of Christ which passes knowledge; that you may be filled with all the fullness of God" (Ephesians 3:17–19). We might compare God in this passage to a boundless ocean and Christ to a mighty Niagara. From the courts of heaven comes a great flood of grace which splashes into the empty thimbles of our lives. The ocean fills us, it spills over and pours out. Common sinners are saved by grace and are made full of the fullness that comes from God alone. Paul knew what it was to live by faith. James knew what it was to live by faith. Living by faith is not being satisfied with the present pardon of sin and a future in heaven. Living by faith is taking all God has said about Himself, ourselves, and the work of His Son, and laboring to live on every one of those realities for the glory of our God. If Christ died to make the presence of God among His people possible, how can it be right for us to say, in practice, that we don't need all that His Son died to give us?

We need to be careful with the biblical teaching regarding God's presence. It is a theme that has been abused by earnest, but mistaken, believers. Thankfully, there are books that can help us here. There is a rich literary heritage on this subject, dating from the seventeenth through the mid-nineteenth century. Sadly, during the last one hundred and fifty years, few helpful books have been written on the topic of God's presence. In the last century, men who are generally careful with doctrine have steered away from the subject of God's experiential presence in His church. However, there are exceptions. In 1991, a congregationalist minister and antiquarian bookseller named Richard Owen Roberts wrote a small book entitled *Revival*. In this book, he defines the term "revival." Revival is not a set of meetings; it is not something you can put on the church calendar. It does not consist of mere excitement or of tears elicited by emotional preaching, and it isn't merely large numbers attending church. Revival is God among His people in an extraordinary way producing extraordinary results.[4] Revival is a true privilege of the Christian because Christ provided for God's presence with His people. This presence among His people is at times experienced in an extraordinary way that produces extraordinary results. Rethinking God biblically also means rethinking the presence of God.

Have you noticed that, in the Bible, God is not always equally distant from His people? There are passages that describe God as far from His people. Other passages describe God as close to them. When we think of the biblical descriptions of God's presence as it relates to us, we can understand them as falling into one of three categories: the essential presence of God, the manifest presence of God, and the cultivated presence of God.[5] The first category of biblical descriptions of God's presence is His essential presence. God's essential presence is simply this: by His nature, God, as deity, is all present. He doesn't travel. There is no place that God is not. God exists everywhere. The mosque where the Muslim prays to his false god has the presence of the true God and the Christian church has the presence of the same true God. This is the essential presence of God—the fact that He is omnipresent. Christian, is that all you want? The same thing the world can have, the essential presence of God?

There is a second category: The manifest presence of God. The manifest presence of God is His essential presence, which has always been, suddenly made obvious. An example of this is found when Solomon built the temple. On the day of the temple dedication, the king prayed. At the end of Solomon's prayer, God answered in a very visible way. God filled the temple with an unapproachable, unbearable glory. The priests fled the temple. Where was God the few moments before the end of the prayer? He was in the Holy of Holies, the outer courts, and everywhere, effortlessly. So what caused this intense, overwhelming presence of the glory of God to happen? Did God come closer? God pulled back the veil, if we might say it in that way, to show what had been there all along. He manifested His glorious presence. The term "manifest presence" is a relational term. It is like being in a room with a child and a parent, and the child has been disobedient. The parent is sitting on one end of the couch, and the child is on the other end of the couch. The parent is staring at the child, waiting for the child to be honest about his wrongdoing. The child knows the parent has caught him, so the child is staring the opposite direction, hoping he can be sent to bed and escape the uneasy feeling in the room. You can be sitting beside someone physically, but relationally you can be a million miles apart.

God is always here, but there are times when He unveils His presence and there is an intimacy and effectiveness that weren't previously experienced. What is the evidence of God's manifest presence? Many people say, "God drew near to me. God was here in our church today. God was in the singing." The one irrefutable evidence that God has manifested His presence, drawn near, is that we become aware of the terrible holiness of God and the inexcusable sin in ourselves.

It is like having a policeman follow you home from church. You pull out of the church parking lot and the policeman pulls up right behind you as you travel down the road. You think, "Well that's not strange. He's just heading down the same road I am." You make a right turn; he makes a right turn. You make a left turn, maybe another turn after that, and the policeman is still following you. You begin to think "Now, this is unusual. Did I forget to come to a complete stop? Was I going too fast? Have I done something wrong?" What has changed to cause you to be keenly aware of the traffic laws? Why do you begin over-scrutinizing everything about your driving? Before the policeman began to follow you, you knew the law existed. However, when the policeman's car is directly behind you, the law is made manifest. In the same way, we know that God exists, we know that He's holy; but when God allows His presence to be felt, and noticed, His holiness and our sin become overwhelming.

The times of God's manifest presence in history have been described in various ways. A Welsh puritan who preached during the sixteen hundreds was ministering in North Wales where the gospel was often rejected at that time. He wrote home after a season during which God seemed to draw near in the preaching. He reported, "The gospel runs like fire in the thatch and across the hills."[6] God drew near and caused the gospel ministry to be effective in a way it had not been before, causing it to spread like a brush fire in the hills. A popular way of describing God's nearness and its impact upon people was to borrow a phrase from the Old Testament, referring to it as the days "of the right hand of the Most High" (Psalm 77:10). Have you ever described your church like that? Have you ever described your life like that? Have you ever been compelled to say something like, "Oh, God, it's as if You rolled up Your sleeve and You stretched Your mighty arm all the way down to my family, and You're working in such a way, it's like these are the days of the right hand of God!"? That is how people describe the experience of God's manifest presence and its impact. When was the last time that we looked at our towns and cities and talked like that?

Any study of the Bible will reveal that God often withdraws His manifest presence from people. In the biblical record, the most frequent purpose for this is gracious judgment. Gracious judgment is when God uses gentle ways to get the attention of His straying people and they continue to disobey, so He increases the severity of the judgment. The purpose of God in this is not destruction, but rescue. It is a gracious, loving discipline. God purposefully allows you to feel the emptiness of living far from Him in disobedience, so that you feel His absence and return to Him. In Hosea 5:15, the idolatry of God's people causes Him to say, "I will return again to My place till they acknowledge their offense. Then they will seek My face; in their affliction they will earnestly seek Me." God withdraws the gracious awareness of His presence and leaves His people to carry on in religion, but without God. The loss of that manifest presence will cause someone—hopefully many—to look around and say, "Where did God go?" Recognizing that God has withdrawn is meant to cause His people to seek Him again. Isaiah 63 was written during another time of spiritual decline among God's people. Isaiah the prophet comes to ask where was the God who brought the people out of Egypt? Where was the One who led them through the wilderness? (Isaiah 63:11–13). Understand this: Isaiah walks with

God. He enjoys the presence of God, but he looks at Israel and says, "It's as if the God who was among us, the one I read about in the books of Moses, isn't with His people anymore." Another example is found in Ezekiel 10. Ezekiel, in a vision, sees the glory of the Lord in the Holy of Holies. Because of the idolatry of the people, God's glory rises out of the Holy of Holies, hovers over the top, and then moves to the outer court. It continues to move to the outer edge of Jerusalem, and then out to the mountains on the horizon. God is so offended by their idols, and He will not give them His wonderful, noticeable, manifest presence until they repent.

Is this withdrawal of God's manifest presence a type of judgment that is limited to the old covenant? After all, in the new covenant, isn't God always equally near to all Christians? It may surprise you to realize that the phenomenon of the withdrawal of God's presence from His people can be found in the New Testament, as well. If not, how do you explain the words of James 4:8, "Draw near to God and He will draw near to you"? There are times when God graciously withdraws His presence so that we might feel the sinfulness of sin, repent, and seek His face. In Revelation 3:19-20, when Christ talks to that compromised, arrogant, self-satisfied church of Laodicea, He says, "As many as I love, I rebuke and chasten. Therefore be zealous and repent. Behold, I stand at the door and knock. If anyone hears My voice and opens the door, I will come in to him and dine with him, and he with Me." Christ, so offended by their arrogance, stepped outside, withdrew His presence, and rebuked the church at Laodicea. In modern language, He tells them, "This is your fault. If you will repent and open the door, I'll come back in, sit down, and we will have supper together." The friendship, the intimacy, the fellowship will be restored, but not until they repent. You can go to church and have a faithful pastor. You can have beneficial Bible studies. You can accumulate a Christian library. You can talk about God with other Christians. You can teach. You can do good deeds. You can evangelize. You can go through all the motions of religion without the nearness of God. In fact, it is possible that His presence has been withdrawn for so long and on such a large scale in your nation, that you believe a distant God is a normal God. But a distant God is not normal. It is judgment.

The third category of the presence of God is the cultivated presence. The cultivated presence of God does not mean you are in any way manipulating God. Just because you do A and B, it does not mean God must do C. You never manipulate God. The cultivated presence of God means you cultivate in yourself the kind of life to which God might be pleased to draw near. Imagine if Queen Elizabeth were to visit America and intended to visit a little town with its regular citizens. The chosen town announces the queen's plans and tells its citizens that if anyone would like to be considered for a visit, they would be given a list of things to do and not do, in order to make the queen's visit pleasant. Anyone serious about having Queen Elizabeth visit their home would get busy removing all the things she dislikes and adding all the things she likes. Now, God has told us in His Word that He will draw near certain people. Are you in earnest about being that kind of person? The wonderful thing about the cultivated presence of God is that an individual Christian can have the joy of God's nearness even if he or she lives in a land from which God has withdrawn. A church might know the cultivated presence of God regardless of the sins of its denomination. An individual church member may experience the cultivated presence of God even if he or she goes to a church where no one else enjoys that privilege. Individuals who enjoy God's presence in this way walk into a room and the aroma of Christ comes with them. It is as if the sweetness of God comes in the room with them and it leaves with them. The deep, calm happiness of those lives is a result of living with the cultivated presence of God.

We need to rethink the biblical teaching regarding the presence of God. We should not take for granted that God is as near to us now as He has ever been or ever will be. There are many passages in the Bible in which God describes the kind of life to which He delights to draw near. If this sounds like a form of legalism to you, it is not. This is not salvation by works that earn God's love. It is, in fact, taking seriously what God tells us about His character and adjusting our lives to please Him, to have a restored fellowship between ourselves and our Savior.

Where do you start if you desire the experiential nearness of God that the new covenant promises? First, be quick to remove from your life all that the Bible reveals as displeasing to God. Whether the sin has been there for a few hours or all your life, if it offends God, get rid of it. Whether it is what the world calls a big sin or a small sin, remove it. Plead with God for the grace to see and repent of it. Second, be willing to add to your life any and every thing in which He delights. Cultivate a humble, hungry, seeking heart and a believing, hoping, and responsive mind. Whatever pleases God, add that to your life. The third element is desire—a patient longing. This patient longing is not a passive kind of patience, as if you were taking a nap. Instead, it is the longing of a lover.

Two examples of this type of longing are helpful. The first is a comment from the seventeenth century pastor, Samuel Rutherford. He viewed his beloved homeland of Scotland and was convinced that he was seeing the presence of God departing from the confused and compromised churches. Rutherford said, "The sea is out, the wind of His Spirit calm; and I cannot buy a wind, or, by requesting the sea, cause it to flow again; only I wait on upon the banks and shore-side, till the Lord send a full sea, that with upsails I may lift up Christ."[7] What a clear picture of biblical longing after God. The sea is out, the tide has receded. Rutherford couldn't make it come back, and neither can we. But we can plead with the Lord to bring it back, and we wait with an aching heart until He does. For another example, imagine a young wife whose husband has been abroad in the military. She receives notice that he is returning from the war. She cleans and organizes the house just the way he likes it. She wants everything to be perfect when he returns. After everything at home is ready, she finds it hard to be patient. She has not been told the exact day of the week that he will arrive. So she goes to the airport every afternoon and watches the planes land. She sees other soldiers get off and run to their wives and children. She knows her husband may not be on that plane, but she cannot help it. She is consumed with a longing that must be patient, yet never indifferent.

Think about the following three sets of questions and consider *your own* spiritual condition. Don't think about your church, family, spouse, or children. The first set of questions is this: Do you want God? Do you want the God the Bible describes? Do you want Him right here, right now? Or would you rather have Him at arm's length, not too close, just where He can be reached in case of need? Do you want Him now or do you want Him a little later, not just yet? Do you really want the God of the Bible?

The second set of questions is this: Do you think that God would be pleased to change His nature? Will He come and dwell among a people who willfully misrepresent Him and hold idolatrously low views of Him? Will He dwell among people who, because of laziness, will not search the Scriptures to make sure the God they have in their minds is the God of Scripture and not just the Jesus of their culture? God has never tolerated idolatry before. Are you counting on Him tolerating it now?

The third set of questions is this: Can there be anything sweeter in the Christian life than having God present among His people in that experiential, noticeable way? He is the most desirable of beings. No one's company is so interesting, captivating, attractive, impressive and beneficial as His.

Begin to carefully consider those passages where God describes the kind of person to whom He delights to draw near. Do not give yourself, or God, any rest until your life has been affected by those passages. You will never do it perfectly, but you must be in earnest. Augustus Toplady wrote a line in one of his hymns about the longing of the Christian for the presence of God. Let it be your cry as well.

Object of my first desire,
Jesus crucified for me;
All to happiness aspire,
Only to be found in Thee.

Lord, it is not life to live
if Thy presence Thou deny;
Lord, if Thou Thy presence give,
'Tis no longer death to die.

[1] John Wesley, *The Life of Rev. John Wesley* (United Kingdom: W. Baynes and Son, 1825), 382.
[2] Amy Carmichael, *God's Missionary* (United States: CLC Publications, 1997), 25.
[3] *New American Standard Bible*. The Lockman Foundation (www.lockman.org), 1995.
[4] Richard Owen Roberts, *Revival,* (np: Richard Owen Roberts Pub, 1991), 16.
[5] I am indebted to Richard Owen Roberts for his teaching on the presence of God.
[6] Eifion Evans, *Fire in the Thatch: The True Nature of Religious Revival* (United Kingdom: Evangelical Press of Wales, 1996), 10.
[7] Samuel Rutherford, *The Letters of Samuel Rutherford 3rd Edition With a Sketch of His Life by Andrew Bonar* (London: The Religious Tract Society, n.d.), 537.

OTHER RESOURCES BY MEDIA GRATIAE

BEHOLD YOUR GOD: RETHINKING GOD BIBLICALLY

by John Snyder

BEHOLD YOUR GOD: THE WEIGHT OF MAJESTY

by John Snyder

LOGIC ON FIRE

The Life and Legacy of Dr. Martyn Lloyd-Jones

PURITAN: ALL OF LIFE TO THE GLORY OF GOD

by Joel Beeke

THE CHURCH

by Jeff Johnson

A PRACTICAL GUIDE TO FAMILY WORSHIP

by Ryan Bush

LIVING WITH THE TRUE GOD: LESSONS FROM JUDGES

by John Snyder

www.mediagratiae.org